# HIP POCKET GUIDE
# TO UNIX ®

# HIP POCKET GUIDE TO UNIX®

*Michele Petrovsky and Tom Parkinson*

## IDG
### BOOKS
##### WORLDWIDE

***IDG Books Worldwide, Inc.***
***An International Data Group Company***

*Foster City, CA ▪ Chicago, IL ▪ Indianapolis, IN ▪ New York, NY*

# Hip Pocket Guide to UNIX®

Published by
**IDG Books Worldwide, Inc.**
An International Data Group Company
919 E. Hillsdale Blvd., Suite 400
Foster City, CA 94404
http: www.idgbooks.com (IDG Books Worldwide Web site)

Library of Congress Catalog Card No.: 98-70240

ISBN: 0-7645-3226-X

Printed in the United States of America

10 9 8 7 6 5 4 3 2 1

1P/QY/QV/ZY/FC

Distributed in the United States by IDG Books Worldwide, Inc.

Distributed by Macmillan Canada for Canada; by Transworld Publishers Limited in the United Kingdom; by IDG Norge Books for Norway; by IDG Sweden Books for Sweden; by Woodslane Pty. Ltd. for Australia; by Woodslane New Zealand Ltd. for New Zealand; by Addison Wesley Longman Singapore Pte Ltd. for Singapore, Malaysia, Thailand, and Indonesia; by Distribuidora Norma S.A.-Colombia for Colombia; by Intersoft for South Africa; by International Thomson Publishing for Germany, Austria, and Switzerland; by Toppan Company Ltd. for Japan; by Distribuidora Cuspide for Argentina; by Livraria Cultura for Brazil; by Ediciencia S.A. for Ecuador; by Addison-Wesley Publishing Company for Korea; by Ediciones ZETA S.C.R. Ltda. for Peru; by WS Computer Publishing Corporation, Inc., for the Philippines; by Unalis Corporation for Taiwan; by Contemporanea de Ediciones for Venezuela; by Computer Book & Magazine Store for Puerto Rico; by Express Computer Distributors for the Caribbean and West Indies. Authorized Sales Agent: Anthony Rudkin Associates for the Middle East and North Africa.

For general information on IDG Books Worldwide's books in the U.S., please call our Consumer Customer Service department at 800-762-2974. For reseller information, including discounts and premium sales, please call our Reseller Customer Service department at 800-434-3422.

For information on where to purchase IDG Books Worldwide's books outside the U.S., please contact our International Sales department at 650-655-3200 or fax 650-655-3297.

For information on foreign language translations, please contact our Foreign & Subsidiary Rights department at 650-655-3021 or fax 650-655-3281.

For sales inquiries and special prices for bulk quantities, please contact our Sales department at 650-655-3200 or write to the address above.

For information on using IDG Books Worldwide's books in the classroom or for ordering examination copies, please contact our Educational Sales department at 800-434-2086.

For press review copies, author interviews, or other publicity information, please contact our Public Relations department at 650-655-3000 or fax 650-655-3299.

For authorization to photocopy items for corporate, personal, or educational use, please contact Copyright Clearance Center, 222 Rosewood Drive, Danvers, MA 01923, or fax 978-750-4470.

™ is a trademark under exclusive license to IDG Books Worldwide, Inc., from International Data Group, Inc.

# ABOUT IDG BOOKS WORLDWIDE

Welcome to the world of IDG Books Worldwide.

IDG Books Worldwide, Inc., is a subsidiary of International Data Group, the world's largest publisher of computer-related information and the leading global provider of information services on information technology. IDG was founded more than 25 years ago and now employs more than 8,500 people worldwide. IDG publishes more than 275 computer publications in over 75 countries (see listing below). More than 60 million people read one or more IDG publications each month.

Launched in 1990, IDG Books Worldwide is today the #1 publisher of best-selling computer books in the United States. We are proud to have received eight awards from the Computer Press Association in recognition of editorial excellence and three from *Computer Currents'* First Annual Readers' Choice Awards. Our best-selling *...For Dummies®* series has more than 30 million copies in print with translations in 30 languages. IDG Books Worldwide, through a joint venture with IDG's Hi-Tech Beijing, became the first U.S. publisher to publish a computer book in the People's Republic of China. In record time, IDG Books Worldwide has become the first choice for millions of readers around the world who want to learn how to better manage their businesses.

Our mission is simple: Every one of our books is designed to bring extra value and skill-building instructions to the reader. Our books are written by experts who understand and care about our readers. The knowledge base of our editorial staff comes from years of experience in publishing, education, and journalism — experience we use to produce books for the '90s. In short, we care about books, so we attract the best people. We devote special attention to details such as audience, interior design, use of icons, and illustrations. And because we use an efficient process of authoring, editing, and desktop publishing our books electronically, we can spend more time ensuring superior content and spend less time on the technicalities of making books.

You can count on our commitment to deliver high-quality books at competitive prices on topics you want to read about. At IDG Books Worldwide, we continue in the IDG tradition of delivering quality for more than 25 years. You'll find no better book on a subject than one from IDG Books Worldwide.

John Kilcullen
CEO
IDG Books Worldwide, Inc.

Steven Berkowitz
President and Publisher
IDG Books Worldwide, Inc.

*Eighth Annual Computer Press Awards ≥1992*

*Ninth Annual Computer Press Awards ≥1993*

*Tenth Annual Computer Press Awards ≥1994*

*Eleventh Annual Computer Press Awards ≥1995*

IDG Books Worldwide, Inc., is a subsidiary of International Data Group, the world's largest publisher of computer-related information and the leading global provider of information services on information technology. International Data Group publishes over 275 computer publications in over 75 countries. Sixty million people read one or more International Data Group publications each month. International Data Group's publications include: ARGENTINA: Buyer's Guide, Computerworld Argentina, PC World Argentina; AUSTRALIA: Australian Macworld, Australian PC World, Australian Reseller News, Computerworld, IT Casebook, Network World, Publish, Webmaster; AUSTRIA: Computerwelt Osterreich, Networks Austria, PC Tip Austria; BANGLADESH: PC World Bangladesh; BELARUS: PC World Belarus; BELGIUM: Data News; BRAZIL: Annuário de Informática, Computerworld, Connections, Macworld, PC Player, PC World, Publish, Reseller News, Supergamepower; BULGARIA: Computerworld Bulgaria, Network World Bulgaria, PC & MacWorld Bulgaria; CANADA: CIO Canada, Client/Server World, ComputerWorld Canada, InfoWorld Canada, NetworkWorld Canada, WebWorld; CHILE: Computerworld Chile, PC World Chile; COLOMBIA: Computerworld Colombia, PC World Colombia; COSTA RICA: PC World Centro America; THE CZECH AND SLOVAK REPUBLICS: Computerworld Czechoslovakia, Macworld Czech Republic, PC World Czechoslovakia; DENMARK: Communications World Danmark, Computerworld Danmark, Macworld Danmark, PC World Danmark, Techworld Denmark; DOMINICAN REPUBLIC: PC World Republica Dominicana; ECUADOR: PC World Ecuador; EGYPT: Computerworld Middle East, PC World Middle East; EL SALVADOR: PC World Centro America; FINLAND: MikroPC, Tietoverkko, Tietoviikko; FRANCE: Distributique, Hebdo, Info PC, Le Monde Informatique, Macworld, Reseaux & Telecoms, WebMaster France; GERMANY: Computer Partner, Computerwoche, Computerwoche Extra, Computerwoche FOCUS, Global Online, Macwelt, PC Welt; GREECE: Amiga Computing, GamePro Greece, Multimedia World; GUATEMALA: PC World Centro America; HONDURAS: PC World Centro America; HONG KONG: Computerworld Hong Kong, PC World Hong Kong, Publish in Asia; HUNGARY: ABCD CD-ROM, Computerworld Szamitastechnika, Internetto online Magazine, PC World Hungary, PC-X Magazin Hungary; ICELAND: Tolvuheimur PC World Island; INDIA: Information Communications World, Information Systems Computerworld, PC World India, Publish in Asia; INDONESIA: InfoKomputer PC World, Komputek Computerworld, Publish in Asia; IRELAND: ComputerScope, PC Live!; ISRAEL: Macworld Israel, People & Computers/Computerworld; ITALY: Computerworld Italia, Macworld Italia, Networking Italia, PC World Italia; JAPAN: DTP World, Macworld Japan, Nikkei Personal Computing, OS/2 World Japan, SunWorld Japan, Windows NT World, Windows World Japan; KENYA: PC World East African; KOREA: Hi-Tech Information, Macworld Korea, PC World Korea; MACEDONIA: PC World Macedonia; MALAYSIA: Computerworld Malaysia, PC World Malaysia, Publish in Asia; MALTA: PC World Malta; MEXICO: Computerworld Mexico, PC World Mexico; MYANMAR: PC World Myanmar; NETHERLANDS: Computer! Totaal, LAN Internetworking Magazine, LAN World Buyers Guide, Macworld Netherlands, Net, WebWereld; NEW ZEALAND: Absolute Beginners Guide and Plain & Simple Series, Computer Buyer, Computer Industry Directory, Computerworld New Zealand, MTB, Network World, PC World New Zealand; NICARAGUA: PC World Centro America; NORWAY: Computerworld Norge, CW Rapport, Datamagasinet, Financial Rapport, Kursguide Norge, Macworld Norge, Multimediaworld Norge, PC World Ekspress Norge, PC World Nettverk, PC World Norge, PC World ProduktGuide Norge; PAKISTAN: Computerworld Pakistan; PANAMA: PC World Panama; PEOPLE'S REPUBLIC OF CHINA: China Computer Users, China Computerworld, China InfoWorld, China Telecom World Weekly, Computer & Communication, Electronic Design China, Electronics Today, Electronics Weekly, Game Software, PC World China, Popular Computer Week, Software Weekly, Software World, Telecom World; PERU: Computerworld Peru, PC World Profesional Peru, PC World SoHo Peru; PHILIPPINES: Click!, Computerworld Philippines, PC World Philippines, Publish in Asia; POLAND: Computerworld Poland, Computerworld Special Report Poland, Cyber, Macworld Poland, Networld Poland, PC World Komputer; PORTUGAL: Cerebro/PC World, Computerworld/Correio Informático, Dealer World Portugal, Mac*In/PC*In Portugal, Multimedia World; PUERTO RICO: PC World Puerto Rico; ROMANIA: Computerworld Romania, PC World Romania, Telecom Romania; RUSSIA: Computerworld Russia, Mir PK, Publish, Seti; SINGAPORE: Computerworld Singapore, PC World Singapore, Publish in Asia; SLOVENIA: Monitor; SOUTH AFRICA: Computing SA, Network World SA, Software World SA; SPAIN: Comunicaciones World España, Computerworld España, Dealer World España, Macworld España, PC World España; SRI LANKA: Infolink PC World; SWEDEN: CAP&Design, Computer Sweden, Corporate Computing Sweden, Internetworld Sweden, it.branschen, Macworld Sweden, MaxiData Sweden, MikroDatorn, Natverk & Kommunikation, PC World Sweden, PCaktiv, Windows World Sweden; SWITZERLAND: Computerworld Schweiz, Macworld Schweiz, PCtip; TAIWAN: Computerworld Taiwan, Macworld Taiwan, NEW ViSiON/Publish, PC World Taiwan, Windows World Taiwan; THAILAND: Publish in Asia, Thai Computerworld; TURKEY: Computerworld Turkiye, Macworld Turkiye, Network World Turkiye, PC World Turkiye; UKRAINE: Computerworld Kiev, Multimedia World Ukraine, PC World Ukraine; UNITED KINGDOM: Acorn User UK, Amiga Action UK, Amiga Computing UK, Apple Talk UK, Computing, Macworld, Parents and Computers UK, PC Advisor, PC Home, PSX Pro, The WEB; UNITED STATES: Cable in the Classroom, CIO Magazine, Computerworld, DOS World, Federal Computer Week, GamePro Magazine, InfoWorld, I-Way, Macworld, Network World, PC Games, PC World, Publish, Video Event, THE WEB Magazine, and WebMaster; online webzines: JavaWorld, NetscapeWorld, and SunWorld Online; URUGUAY: InfoWorld Uruguay; VENEZUELA: Computerworld Venezuela, PC World Venezuela; and VIETNAM: PC World Vietnam.
3/24/97

# CREDITS

**Acquisitions Editor**
Juliana Aldous

**Development Editor**
Susannah Pfalzer

**Technical Editor**
Brian Lalor

**Copy Editor**
Timothy Borek

**Production Coordinator**
Susan Parini

**Book Designer**
Kurt Krames

**Graphics and Production Specialist**
Jude Levinson

**Quality Control Specialists**
Mick Arellano
Mark Schumann

**Illustrators**
Hector Mendoza
Linda Marosek

**Proofreader**
Sarah Fraser

**Indexer**
Rebecca Plunkett

# ABOUT THE AUTHORS

**Michele Petrovsky** received her Bachelor of Arts in Spanish and Russian and Master of Science in Computer Information Science from the University of Pittsburgh. She has worked as a freelance author and editor and has taught at the university and community college levels. She has published books on upgrading and repairing networks, Internet Information Server, and dynamic HTML.

Michele lives on a Christmas tree farm (really) just north of Wilmington, Delaware, with three cats and the occasional visiting deer, possum, raccoon, and skunk. In her spare time, she enjoys science fiction, *Star Trek*, gardening, and Tai Chi. Michele welcomes feedback from readers at petrovsk@voicenet.com.

**Tom Parkinson's** two professional backgrounds—librarianship and data processing—strengthen his writing. Tom polished his research skills during several years as a librarian at the collegiate level. He has extensive programming experience and is currently the System Administrator for the libraries of Delaware County Community College.

Tom holds two Master of Science degrees, in Library Science and in Computer/Information Science, both from the University of Pittsburgh. He enjoys bicycle touring, woodworking, and playing electric blues and rock guitar. You can chat with Tom at tpark@voicenet.com.

*To Tom's sister Denise, environmental attorney extraordinaire and our favorite technophobe, and also to our friend Harry.*

# PREFACE

UNIX has been around for what in data processing amounts to eons. It certainly is the veteran among operating systems you're likely to encounter; none of the versions of Windows has anything approaching UNIX's track record. Unfortunately, UNIX's reputation for being cryptic and arcane is almost as firmly entrenched. That reputation is what this book tries to dispel. We enjoy UNIX. As a matter of fact, we consider it to be one of the few forms of computer language that can claim to even begin to approach the breadth, flexibility, and power of expression of human languages.

Just as you had to learn to recognize objects and events in the real world before you learned to talk, before learning UNIX you'll have to learn a few other things. We've structured this book in a way that helps you to learn UNIX quickly.

## How This Book Is Organized

Section 1 discusses all the concepts you'll need to absorb in order to be able to work effectively in UNIX. For example, this first section of the book dissects how UNIX handles files, how it controls access to its file system, how to construct UNIX commands, and how to use those commands in the UNIX form of batch programming known as *shell scripts*.

Section 2 presents descriptions and examples of 95 UNIX commands. We've tried to include not only the most widely used UNIX directives in this section but also some more advanced commands you're likely to encounter as you learn more about UNIX. (This book, however, does not cover the most advanced commands, syntaxes, and techniques of UNIX.) So, you'll not only find commands here that allow you to compare, control, list, and massage files, but you'll also learn how to use commands that do such things as communicate with remote UNIX machines.

This book also provides a glossary and a bibliography that give you more sources to turn to about UNIX.

## Who Should Read This Book

Anyone involved in the configuration, maintenance, or management of a UNIX system, whatever its size or flavor, can benefit from this book. Even if you're a beginner or intermediate user, with questions such as "Is there a way I can run several UNIX commands at once?" you'll find help here.

# Conventions Used in This Book

*Hip Pocket Guide to UNIX* follows a few conventions. Anytime we use a technical term for the first time, it will be spelled out in *italics*, followed immediately by an italicized acronym for the term, if any exists.

Similarly, every time this book presents

- a system or application prompt to the user
- the name of a command

that text is shown in a `monospace` code font. Commands or other strings you must type appear in a **bold** font.

Every command covered by *Hip Pocket Guide to UNIX* begins with a short description of the command's function. Then we give you a summary of the syntax that must be applied to the command. Next, you see a real-world example of the command at work. We wrap up coverage of the command with a description of any quirks or characteristics you need to know about, and refer you to other related commands.

While we offer all basic UNIX commands, we don't

- identify, on a per-command basis, the particular versions of UNIX in which our real-world examples will work. We have, however, successfully tested each and every such example on both a Hewlett-Packard Series 9000 minicomputer running HP-UX v10.20 and an AT&T PC 6300 Plus running System V UNIX v2.0.
- cover every option available for every command. We omit the unusually obscure ones. (Yes, there is some basis for UNIX's reputation.)

Enjoy your UNIX journey!

# ACKNOWLEDGMENTS

No book is the product of only a few people. So, it's impossible to thank everyone who contributed to this one. But we feel we must mention Juliana Aldous and Susannah Pfalzer at IDG Books Worldwide, for their enthusiasm.

# CONTENTS AT A GLANCE

# TABLE OF CONTENTS

# UNIX BASICS

These first few dozen pages of *Hip Pocket Guide to UNIX* discuss the concepts upon which UNIX is built, and which you must understand in order to be able to use it effectively. The concepts we cover in this section include

- significant flavors of UNIX, including System V, Berkeley, and Linux, as well as how the operating system evolved into these flavors, and the features they do and do not share

- the UNIX command line environment, including using pipes and redirection in those command lines

- the UNIX kernel and its control of tasks, users, and hardware

- the UNIX shell and its role as both user interface and programming environment

## Significant Flavors of UNIX

UNIX, like most software, isn't monolithic. It exists in a number of varieties. The differences between these varieties, or *flavors*, as they're often called, are seldom glaring. To an end-user, the differences may not at first be apparent at all. But as you become more involved with, and adept at, using UNIX, those differences come to light and may affect what you're trying to do. So, we'll give you a leg up, and introduce the most significant flavors of UNIX here.

We begin with a brief look at the evolution of UNIX and those flavors. Then we distinguish between features that remain constant among them, and those that vary from flavor to flavor. Finally, we offer personality profiles of three of the most widely used UNIX versions: System V, Berkeley, and Linux.

### The evolution of UNIX

UNIX made its appearance in the early 1970s at Bell Labs in Princeton, New Jersey. The goal of the designers of UNIX was to create an operating system that was first and foremost a flexible programming environment. That was a decidedly different path than the one followed in operating system development up to that point. Before

UNIX the goal of operating systems had been maximizing the efficiency with which hardware was used. The fact that almost all operating systems prior to UNIX were written in assembly language is evidence of this emphasis on efficient use of hardware; assembly language is only one step above the zeroes and ones that are all computers truly understand. Assembly language, because it must deal directly with such specifics of hardware architecture as word size, registers, stacks, and so on, is decidedly nonportable. For example, assembly language code written with the structure of an Intel processor in mind simply would not run on a platform that relies on a Motorola chip.

The earliest version of UNIX was written in assembly language for the PDP-7 mini-computer from Digital Equipment Corporation (DEC). But it wasn't long before the great bulk of *kernel,* or core functions — between 90 and 95 percent — were rewritten in the C language. This use of C is what gives UNIX both its portability and its great flexibility. C combines the strengths of assembly language with the more sophisticated programming constructs ordinarily only available in high-level languages such as FORTRAN or Pascal.

UNIX's ongoing close ties to academia began in 1973, when AT&T in effect donated the OS to a number of universities and colleges. This, taken together with the fact that UNIX distributions then and now contained the system's complete source code, in turn gave rise to the ongoing enhancement of UNIX by academic institutions. For example, a 1978 version of UNIX was introduced that included such new features as

- support for files up to one gigabyte in size (Remember how long it took DOS to be able to address anything beyond 540MB?)
- standardized *input/output,* or I/O, routines
- sophisticated typesetting utilities

These features and more were further enhanced and added to by members of the Computer Science Department at the University of California at Berkeley. In this way, Berkeley UNIX (also known as *BSD* for Berkeley System Development) came to be. Many of these features also characterize many of today's UNIX flavors, such as

- a text- and line-oriented editor called *vi*
- a new user interface called the *C shell*
- a terminal capabilities or *termcap* file, which identifies and details the operating characteristics of I/O devices
- *virtual,* which is swappable-so-fast-you-think-you-have-more-than-there-really-is, memory
- built-in networking

## Constant features

From the start, UNIX has always offered features now recognized as essential to any *multitasking, multiuser* operating system. Let's define those two terms, since they are among the most important of the features that remain constant across all flavors of UNIX.

A multitasking operating system is one that can juggle processes in and out of a *central processing unit,* or CPU, so quickly and efficiently that the processor can execute several tasks at once. A multiuser system is one that can handle a number of simultaneous user sessions. For instance, Windows NT Server can act as a multiuser OS; Windows 3.*x* cannot. In addition to being the first, and in our opinion still the premier, multitasking, multiuser OS, UNIX of whatever stripe gives you such significant tools as

- a hierarchical file system that allows you to organize data easily and efficiently
- a system of file access permissions that allows you to control whether individuals or groups can read, modify, or run both files and, in the case of read or write permissions, directories and subdirectories
- a system of user IDs and passwords that allows you to tailor and monitor access to your machine
- the ability to run processes in the background, that is, without tying up your computer
- the ability to schedule jobs in a number of different ways
- built-in networking tools

## System V

One early flavor of UNIX was System V. The direct descendant of the original Bell Labs UNIX, System V is characterized by

- an improved means of updating files, intended to minimize the risk of data corruption due to system crashes
- interprocess communications that rely on such techniques as shared memory and named pipes (more about pipes in a bit)

## Berkeley

4.2 BSD, the most recent Berkeley release to gain wide acceptance and use, features

- faster file access than either earlier Berkeley or System V flavors
- support for filenames much longer than the 14 characters that had previously been available under BSD
- virtual memory
- networking based on the concept of *sockets*; think of sockets as virtual, rather than physical, connections between sender and receiver

## Linux

Linux, a version of UNIX originally written for the PC by Linus Torvald and maintained as a labor of love by programmers and engineers worldwide, is characterized by

- the ability to run on Intel CPUs 386 and higher
- the ability to run on more powerful machines such as SPARC workstations and DEC Alphas
- support for a great variety of application software, including servers, clients, emulators, editors, programming and development tools, games, networking, and Web publishing and surfing

While currently also commercially available, Linux was for some time and remains, in some of its versions, freeware.

# The UNIX Command Line Environment

While there are windowing systems and interfaces available for UNIX, the operating system's default user interface is called the *shell.* Any UNIX shell relies on *command lines* to allow a user to converse with the operating system. The cue that UNIX gives a user to tell him or her that the OS is ready to chat, such as that shown in Figure 1-1, differs depending on who the user is.

```
Value of TERM has been set to "unknown".
WARNING:  YOU ARE SUPERUSER !!
#
#
```

**Figure 1-1** *This is the prompt that UNIX gives to what it calls the superuser.*

If the user of the moment is what's called the *superuser* or *root* — that is, someone with such extensive file access and program execution permissions that he or she can, in effect, do whatever they wish — the shell tells that user that UNIX is ready to converse by displaying a pound sign (#) as a prompt. If, on the other hand, the user is anyone else, however UNIX knowledgeable, the shell displays a different prompt, such as the one you see in Figure 1-2 — usually a dollar sign ($).

```
                    Hewlett-Packard Company
                    3000 Hanover Street
                    Palo Alto, CA 94304 U.S.A.

Rights for non-DOD U.S. Government Departments and Agencies are as set
forth in FAR 52.227-19(c)(1,2).
$
```

**Figure 1-2** *All users but the superuser see this prompt when they log in.*

Whichever prompt UNIX gives you, it's telling you, "I expect you to give me some sort of command to carry out now." In conveying your wishes to UNIX at the command line, you must follow certain rules:

- **Name of the command.** On any UNIX command line, the first thing you type must be the name of the command you want UNIX to execute.

- **Location of the command.** If the command you want UNIX to carry out is neither in the directory in which you're currently working, or in what's called the *search path* (a list of directories to which you're given access when your user account is set up), you must enter not just the command name, but its full path name, as in

  /sbin/fdisk

- **Options.** If you want to tweak the way in which UNIX carries out the command whose name you've just entered, you must tell the OS by entering the specific wrinkle or wrinkles, known to UNIX as *options*, after the command name, and usually preceded by a dash ( – ).

- **Arguments.** If you want UNIX to do its command thing on a particular body of data, you must ordinarily tell it so specifically, after you've entered the command name and any options you might wish it to use.

What do we mean by ordinarily? Some UNIX commands automatically take their input from what's called *standard input*, and deliver their output to what's called *standard output*. Standard input means default source of input and is almost always associated with the keyboard. Standard output means default destination for output, and is almost always affiliated with the monitor. You can change these defaults; we discuss how to do that in the sections on redirection.

Take a look at Figure 1-3 for an example of a complete, correct, and commonplace UNIX command line that uses all the elements described here and foregoes either standard input, standard output, or redirection.

```
$
$ ls -l /etc
```

**Figure 1-3** *This UNIX command produces a listing of files in the current directory.*

# Using Pipes with UNIX Command Lines

UNIX, designed to be a programming and development environment, bends over backwards to make your life easy, at least as far as offering you several ways to get a job done. Where command lines are concerned, UNIX gives you two ways to combine commands on a single line.

If all you want to do is save yourself some typing, you can string commands together on one command line simply by separating them with the semicolon ( ; ) character (see Figure 1-4).

```
$
$ cd /usr; ls -l
total 118
lrwxr-xr-t    1 root      sys          8 Jun 10   1996 adm -> /var/adm
dr-xr-xr-x    6 bin       bin       8192 Jun 10   1996 bin
dr-xr-xr-x    7 bin       bin       1024 Jun 10   1996 bms
dr-xr-xr-x    5 bin       bin       1024 Jun 10   1996 ccs
dr-xr-xr-x   25 bin       bin       1024 Jun 10   1996 conf
dr-xr-xr-x   10 bin       bin       1024 Jun 10   1996 contrib
dr-xr-xr-x    9 bin       bin       1024 Jun 10   1996 dt
dr-xr-xr-x    5 bin       bin       1024 Jun 10   1996 etc
dr-xr-xr-x    7 bin       bin       1024 Jun 10   1996 examples
dr-xr-xr-x    2 bin       bin       1024 Jun 10   1996 hpC2400
dr-xr-xr-x   17 bin       bin       4096 Jun 10   1996 include
lr-xr-xr-t    1 root      sys         14 Jun 10   1996 keysh -> /usr/lib/ke
h
dr-xr-xr-x    9 bin       bin       1040 Nov  5 09:35 lbin
dr-xr-xr-x   32 bin       bin       6144 Nov  5 09:35 lib
drwxrwxrwx    7 bin       bin       1024 Jun 10   1996 local
drwxr-xr-x    2 root      root      8192 Jun 10   1996 lost+found
lrwxrwxrwt    1 root      sys          9 Jun 10   1996 mail -> /var/mail
lr-xr-xr-t    1 root      sys         14 Jun 10   1996 man -> /usr/share/ma
lr-xr-xr-t    1 root      sys         13 Jun 10   1996 netls -> /var/opt/i
dr-xr-xr-x    7 bin       bin       1024 Jun 10   1996 newconfig
lrwxrwxrwt    1 root      sys          9 Jun 10   1996 news -> /var/news
dr-xr-xr-x    4 bin       bin       1024 Jun 10   1996 obam
```

**Figure 1-4** *With a single line, we've carried out both a change of directory and a listing of files in the new directory.*

If, on the other hand, you want to automatically make the output of one command accessible as input to a second, you must do more. You must, as Figure 1-5 shows, do the following:

■ Use the pipe symbol ( | ).

■ Place the command that will be the source of input to the left of the pipe symbol.

■ Place the command that will be the receiver of that input to the right of the pipe symbol.

```
$
$ ls -l | grep local
drwxrwxrwx    7 bin       bin       1024 Jun 10   1996 local
$
```

**Figure 1-5** *This command line sends the output of the* ls *command to the command* grep, *which then looks for a match in that output with the string* local. *As a result, only one line of final output is produced.*

As the previous example indicates, the output of the ls command needs no further formatting or preparation by you. Rather, UNIX hands that output directly to the command grep, which immediately accepts it and proceeds to do its thing — finding patterns within the output ls generated.

You can string as many commands together in this fashion as you like, assuming, of course, that the output of anything to the left of a pipe symbol will make sense as input to the command to the right of that symbol. Failing to observe this commonsensical caveat can produce results such as those in Figure 1-6, in which the command echo (which, as its name implies, just repeats whatever is fed to it) has nothing with which to work.

```
$
$
$ ls -l | grep local | echo
$
```

**Figure 1-6** *This time,* grep *found no match in the directory listing for the string* local. *As a result,* echo *has nothing to say.*

# Redirecting Input and Output of UNIX Command Lines

Ordinarily when you run a program, you give little thought to where input for it will come from, or to where the program's output will be sent. It was to facilitate this "one-less-thing-to-worry-about" approach that the UNIX concepts of standard input, standard output, and standard error were fashioned. But UNIX doesn't force you to accept its default means of deriving input or directing output. Remember, this OS was designed with flexibility in mind. That flexibility is reflected in the ability to do what old UNIX hands call *redirection.*

To fully understand redirection, we must first introduce another concept — devices as files.

UNIX goes a step further than other widely known operating systems, such as the Windows family, in handling the physical components of a computer. In addition to dealing with these components strictly as the sites of processing or storage, UNIX can approach them as if they were files. In fact, there is a standard portion of the UNIX file system, called the *device directory,* or /dev, in which a separate file is maintained for every component of a machine. Every major subdivision of a hard drive; every other type of disk drive; tape drives; ports, whether serial or parallel; memory; you name it — UNIX has a file for it in /dev.

These files are of two general types:

- Character-special
- Block-special

The file type associated with a device is an indication of how the device handles data. Character-special devices ordinarily move bits in a continuous, unsegmented stream. Block-special devices work with data chunks of predefined sizes and characteristics. Even more important is the fact that, by being able to deal with hardware devices as if they were files, we can easily grab data from them or zap it to them.

Three symbol combinations are used to access data. These are

- the greater-than symbol ( > ), used for output redirection
- a double greater-than symbol ( >> ), the append indicator
- the less-than symbol ( < ), used for input redirection

That's all there is to it. With these three symbols and a general knowledge of the names assigned to hardware components in the /dev directory of a given UNIX machine, you can tailor input sources and output destinations in a variety of ways, as described below.

## Output redirection

Let's use the command ls as our first example of output redirection. ls, the UNIX analog to MS-DOS's dir command, can produce several sets of details about files. Ordinarily ls does just what the figure below shows — sends its output, a listing of files in the directory in which you're currently working, to the screen.

```
$ ls
adm         dt          lbin        netls       pub         tsm
bin         etc         lib         newconfig   sam         vue
bms         examples    local       news        sbin
ccs         hpC2400     lost+found  obam        share
conf        include     mail        old         spool
contrib     keysh       man         preserve    tmp
$
```

**Figure 1-7** *This is how* ls *presents information to you unless you ask it for a more detailed display.*

But what if you want a printout of the files in your directory? No problem; just use a bit of redirection of output. That is, tell ls to send its output somewhere other than it normally would — in this case, the printer, as shown in Figure 1-8.

```
#
# ls > /dev/lp
#
```

**Figure 1-8** *We've redirected our file listing to the printer "file."*

With the addition of a single simple symbol, >, and a device name, /dev/lp, to the command line, you've taken control of ls and caused it to work to meet your needs even better. Think of what you can do now. If, for instance, your printouts ordinarily go to a printer down the hall, you can, with output redirection, make your life easier, and send hard copy to the printer next to your cubicle instead.

How about a snazzier use of output redirection? Assuming there's appropriate cabling in place, you can use redirects to exchange data between computers, regardless of the underlying operating systems or application suites present. All you need to do is to redirect output to the serial port of the source machine and have the destination machine listening for bits arriving at its serial port. Several years ago, we used just this technique to transfer large files between two machines that everyone told us were incompatible and incapable of communicating with one another — an

AT&T UNIX PC and a Burroughs mainframe. The file transfer worked like a charm, with a common line like the one in Figure 1-9 at the PC end.

```
$
$
$
$ ls -l > /dev/rmt/c0t1d0
$
```

**Figure 1-9** *Keep in mind that device designations like the one shown here can differ from one environment to another.*

There's another important wrinkle to output redirection. Let's go back to our `ls` example for a moment. What if you want to keep a history, stored in a disk file over a period of weeks, of the contents of the directory `goodstuf`? Simple output redirection using

```
ls /goodstuf > /usr/myhome/filehist
```

will work the first time around. This command line will take a listing of the `goodstuf` directory and place that listing in a file called `filehist` in the directory `/usr/myhome`. But after that first redirect, this command line would backfire on you. Rather than creating a cumulative listing of the `goodstuf` directory, this command would instead create a new listing each time you run it, replacing all previous output in `filehist`. So much for your attempts at monitoring over time! The solution, as shown in Figure 1-10 (of course UNIX has a solution — it has answers for just about everything), is to use the append indicator, the double greater-than symbol, instead of the simple redirect.

```
# ls -l > lst4book
#
# ls -l lst4book
-rw-rw-rw-   1 root          sys           1513 Jan 10 14:20 lst4book
#
# ls -l >> lst4book
#
# ls -l lst4book
-rw-rw-rw-   1 root          sys           3026 Jan 10 14:21 lst4book
#
#
```

**Figure 1-10** *That's two greater-than symbols, not just one, in the third command line here.*

If you compare the output of the second command line in Figure 1-10 to that of the fourth, you'll see different numbers in column five of each. That tells you that the append operation we carried out succeeded. In a long listing like that shown in this Figure, column 5 represents the size in bytes of files. So, appending caused the file `lst4book` very nearly to double in size.

Using a command line like that just illustrated causes output to be placed at the end of the named file. If the file doesn't exist yet, not to worry. As we said, UNIX has an answer for nearly everything. If you use the append indicator with a name that represents no existing file, UNIX will simply create the file, as it did when you carried out a simple redirect.

One last point about output redirection, though no doubt you've deduced it already: while it won't give you an error, using append, rather than simple output redirection, makes no sense with anything other than files on disk.

## Input redirection

Only the less-than symbol can be used to grab input for a command from somewhere other than where the command would expect to find that input. There's no equivalent to append on this side of the redirect fence. But even simple input redirection can be quite handy, as Figure 1-11 illustrates. First, it used the file lst4book as its source of input. Second, it presented us not only with the number of lines in the file that contain the string we indicated but with the lines themselves.

```
#
# grep -n lst4book < lst4book
14:-rw-rw-rw-  1 root        sys             0 Jan 10 14:20 lst4book
38:-rw-rw-rw-  1 root        sys          1513 Jan 10 14:20 lst4book
#
#
```

**Figure 1-11** *This* grep *command, as we've combined it with input redirection, did two jobs for the price of one.*

Let's say that you've written a UNIX program (called a *shell script* — we discuss shell scripts in the section, "Shell as Programming Environment") that entertains you and your friends by generating lofty-sounding jargon. When it's fine-tuned, the program will prompt users for input. But for now, while you're testing and honing it, you want it to take its input from a small file in your home directory. Rather than modify the shell script and then have to change it again when you're done polishing it, you can simply test it with input redirection. A command line like

```
jargon < testjarg
```

would work just fine for such trial runs.

# Shell and Kernel

In the previous section, we mention shell scripts — UNIX's analogs to batch programs like those with which so many of us became familiar in our DOS days. Earlier on, we talk about UNIX in the role of programming environment and the effect of that role on the nature of user interfaces to UNIX. All these questions bear on the way in which UNIX is constructed — as a core or *kernel*, surrounded by a user interface or *shell* (see Figure 1-12).

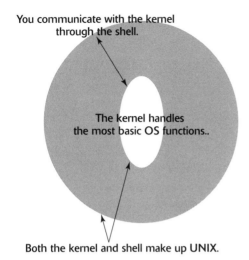

You communicate with the kernel through the shell.

The kernel handles the most basic OS functions..

Both the kernel and shell make up UNIX.

**Figure 1-12** *The relationship between, and interaction of, the shell and the kernel gives UNIX its personality.*

# The UNIX kernel

*Core, essence, heart, soul* — all these words describe the UNIX kernel (or indeed, the kernel of any operating system; the term's no longer confined to being used in a UNIX context). Put simply, the UNIX kernel does all the basic and critical work of the operating system. For instance, the kernel

- controls user access by checking every login attempt for a legitimate user ID and password
- manages program execution, allocating memory and CPU time to every process, and assigning priorities to them
- manages the file system
- runs and manages the shell, through which you converse with the OS
- carries out the exchange of data between memory, processor, and source or destination devices like printers, tapes, and so on

Right now you're probably saying to yourself (and rightly so), "So what? All operating systems do that stuff." That's true, of course, but not all operating systems are multiuser, multitasking systems. And even those that are, whether their designers admit it or not, are modeled upon the original such system — UNIX.

## The UNIX kernel and multiple users

Since it can offer its services to more than one person simultaneously, UNIX — that is, the kernel — must be able to juggle

- monitoring the number of active sessions, so as to be ready to receive commands from them
- terminating sessions as users finish their work
- creating new sessions as users log on
- tracking sessions and the physical devices from which they take place for administrative information (that is, keeping an eye on who is doing what, from where, and with an effect on what else)

If the kernel is doing its job properly, and if it isn't overburdened, every one of these user-related tasks takes place so that each user feels he has the operating system's undivided attention.

## The UNIX kernel and multitasking

Even more demanding a juggling act than handling several users at once is the kernel's need to manage a number of tasks, or as they're called in UNIX-ese, *processes*, simultaneously.

Notice that we say "manage" rather than "run." Neither UNIX nor any other real-world operating system is truly capable of *parallel processing*, that is, doing several things at the same time. But UNIX does excel at making it seem as if it can. What the OS does is use a form of time sharing to balance and satisfy as well as it can the multitude of demands upon its single processor. And it's the kernel that has the responsibility for UNIX's time-sharing scheme.

The kernel keeps a list of processes that have been submitted to it for execution. It assigns a tiny bit of CPU time to each member of that list, in the sequence in which jobs were placed in the list. What's more, the kernel runs through this *process queue*, as it's called, a number of times. In other words, it's rare for a process to run to completion the first time the kernel notices it and gives it access to the CPU. Rather, processes commonly are swapped in and out several times before they're done.

Let's add another complication to the kernel's responsibility for process management. Sometimes, one task can automatically generate another. For instance, the command `wall`, which stands for "write to all," sends the same message to all users currently logged in. But in order to send the message, it must first determine who's out there. Ergo, one process, known in UNIX circles as the *parent*, creates or spawns another process, the *child*. And who keeps track of which processes are related to which others, and in what way? You guessed it — the kernel.

## The UNIX kernel and control of hardware

In a nutshell, if you'll forgive the pun, there's only one way for you to communicate with hardware on a UNIX machine — through the kernel. It's the kernel that, through small modules of canned, low-level code known as *system calls*, carries out all hardware manipulation, including such commonplace tasks as

- opening and closing files (disk access)
- accepting input from keyboard or mouse
- sending output to monitor or printer

  So, if you create a new copy of an existing file with a command like

```
cp oldfile newfile
```

it isn't the `cp` command itself that manipulates disk storage to create the new version of old data. Rather, `cp` calls the kernel routines appropriate to doing that. Then those routines handle the replication of the information in one file and the placement of the copy into another.

This reliance of UNIX commands on system calls illustrates another relationship — that between the kernel and the shell, your means of talking to UNIX. Let's examine that relationship further.

# The UNIX shell

The shell is itself a program, run automatically by the kernel for every user each time he or she logs in. It's the shell's job to

- let you know it's ready to go to work, that is, to allow you to enter commands
- accept commands you type
- pass any requests the commands entail for data to the kernel
- accept what the kernel produces as a result
- return those results to you
- let you know that it's ready to move on to the next command

The first and last of these, the shell does through signaling you with a special character known as a *prompt*. Depending on the flavor of UNIX in which you're working, that prompt will, for most users, be

- a dollar sign ( $ ) for System V and other Bell-derivative versions of UNIX
- a percent sign ( % ) for Berkeley-based UNIX

These differences in prompts reflect a more basic difference between System V and Berkeley — the fact that they use shells of a slightly different nature.

## *The Bourne shell*

This most widely-used UNIX user interface and command interpreter, named for its author, Stephen Bourne, most often resides on System V UNIX versions, but it can be used even on systems running Berkeley or other flavors of UNIX not originating from Bell Labs. Like all UNIX shells, the Bourne shell does the following:

- Relies on special characters, called *metacharacters*, as a form of shorthand

---

- Keeps a set of variables, called *shell* or *environment variables*, which denote the characteristics of the current shell session
- Keeps a file, called a *profile* and known in formal UNIX terms as `.profile`, for every user who has been defined to it, containing the characteristics of that user's account and the conditions to be applied to that user's sessions

### The C shell

Perhaps the best way to compare the C shell, found in Berkeley-based versions of UNIX and the Bourne shell, is through Table 1-1, which outlines the similarities and differences between the two. The C shell differs from the Bourne shell in the prompt it presents to most users, in how it handles setting environment variables, and in some of its configuration files.

**Table 1-1** *C Shell and Bourne shell comparison*

| This item . . . | Appears in the shell . . . | And indicates . . . |
| --- | --- | --- |
| The metacharacter ? | Bourne and C | Any single character can be substituted. For example, if you wanted a listing of all files whose names began with *w* and ended with *w*, and that had any one character in between, you could use this command:<br>`ls w?w` |
| The metacharacter * | Bourne and C | Anywhere from none through one to as many as you want characters can be substituted for it. So, if you need a listing of all files whose names start with *w*, end with *w*, and have any number of characters in between, you could use this command:<br>`ls w*w` |
| The metacharacter & | Bourne and C | The command to which it's attached should be run in the background. |
| The metacharacter \| | Bourne and C | The output of the command to the left of the pipe serves as input for the command to the right. |
| The metacharacter < | Bourne and C | A nonstandard source of input. |
| The metacharacter > | Bourne and C | A nonstandard destination for output. |

| This item . . . | Appears in the shell . . . | And indicates . . . |
|---|---|---|
| The metacharacter pair [ ] | Bourne and C | A range of characters to be used. So, if you executed this `ls` command: `ls [abcd]?e` |
| | | you'd get results including files named things like `aae`, `ale`, `bfe`, and so on, but you wouldn't get any output like `eae`. |
| The shell variable HOME | Bourne and C | The full path name of your home directory, that is, the directory in that you are placed when you log in. |
| The shell variable IFS | Bourne and C | The internal field separator the shell will use, that is, the characters that may be used to separate words in a command line. |
| The shell variable LOGNAME | Bourne and C | The name under which a user is logged in. |
| The shell variable MAIL | Bourne and C | The name of the directory in which your email will be placed. |
| The shell variable PATH | Bourne and C | The list of directories and subdirectories the shell will search to find program files for you, and whose full names you therefore don't have to specify when requesting those files or programs. |
| The shell variable PS1 | Bourne and C | The first and most frequent prompt string the shell will use. |
| The shell variable PS2 | Bourne and C | The prompt string the shell will use if you start a new command line without first finishing the one you're on. |
| The shell variable TERM | Bourne and C | The kind of terminal you're using, and therefore, things like how the shell should interpret your pressing function and other special keys. |
| The file .profile | Bourne | Your account's characteristics, and any commands that should be executed when you log in. |

*Continued*

---

**Table 1-1** *Continued*

| This item . . . | Appears in the shell . . . | And indicates . . . |
|---|---|---|
| The file .login | C | Any commands to be carried out when you log in. |
| The file .cshrc | C | Shell session characteristics. |
| Commands of the form VARIABLE=value | Bourne | Setting or resetting an environment variable, as in TERM=vt220 Setting the terminal type to that of a VT220 emulation. |
| Commands of the form setenv VARIABLE value | C | Setting or resetting an environment variable. |
| The prompt $ | Bourne | The OS is ready to chat with an average user. |
| The prompt % | C | The OS is ready to chat with an average user. |
| The prompt # | Bourne and C | The system is waiting to talk with the superuser. |

# Shell as Programming Environment

Like many operating systems, UNIX allows you to string a number of commands together in a single file and to execute that file as if it were a program. In fact, it is a program — one that will carry out the commands you've placed in it, in the order in which you put them there.

Being a bit more elegant than many OSs, UNIX calls these files *shell scripts*, not batch files.

Before we go any further, you should know that every script, large or small, in this section was written and tested on a Hewlett-Packard machine — an HP 9000/816, under HP-UX 10.2. All our scripts reflect the syntax that platform requires.

Shell scripts can be quite simple. Take a look at this one, which is no more than a slightly chattier version of an existing UNIX command.

```
echo Here are all the good folks
echo who are logged in right now.
who
```

This three-line script produces output like that in Figure 1-13. By the way, the cat command, which in this Figure shows you the contents of our little script, can also be used to concatenate files. In fact, that's where it got its name.

```
#
# cat progenv_1
echo Here are all the good folks
echo Who are logged in right now.
who
#
# ./progenv_1
Here are all the good folks
Who are logged in right now.
root        ttyp3        Jan 28 17:07
```

**Figure 1-13**  *One common use of shell scripts is to dress up UNIX commands,
as we've done here.*

There are two ways to cause this output to be produced. The first is to make the
script name an argument to the sh command, like this:

sh chattywho

The sh command is actually the name of the shell program. If you are using a
different shell (such as the Bourne shell), a different command starts the script.

This command line causes the shell to

- create a new, child process called chattywho

- carry out the commands in chattywho

- when that's done, return control to the parent process, your original shell session

Why, you're probably asking, can't we simply run the command chattywho
directly? Well, we can. But first, we must prepare the script for execution. Like all
newly-created files in a UNIX file system, shell scripts are assigned the default
permissions read and write, meaning we can look at or modify them. But no new
UNIX file comes into the world with execute permission. So, to make chattywho into
a true program, we must explicitly give it executability. We can do this with the
command chmod, which stands for *change mode*. Here's an example:

chmod +x chattywho

Once this command line is carried out, chattywho is ready to roll, directly from
the prompt, without any help from sh.

Shell scripts can accomplish much more than the playful tinkering we did with
chattywho. But to do so, they must call upon some of the same logic structures that
programming languages like Basic, C, and others use.

In any programming language, there are two broad categories of such constructs:

- Decision-making statements or structures

- Repetitive or looping structures

Let's look at how UNIX shell scripts handle both of these.

## Making decisions

There are two ways for any programming language to make a decision or choice
between alternatives. In formal language, these are known as *single-branching* and
*multiple-branching* structures. Most frequently, single-branching decisions (that is, ones

---

of a yes/no, right/left, forward/backward nature) are programmed with what are known as if *statements*. UNIX shell scripts use if statements too.

## If *statements in scripts*

Let's say you want to write a shell script that will compare files and delete any duplicates. You'd need the following items:

■ The command cmp, which compares two files. When you use the command's s option, it makes sure they're exactly the same.

■ A way to tell UNIX to remove one of the files if duplication is discovered.

■ A way to tell UNIX which file to discard.

Take a look at the following shell script. Then glance at it again in Table 1-2, which explains it.

```
# shell script vacuum
# This script finds and gets rid of duplicate files.
# Use it like this.
# vacuum filename other_filename
if cmp -s $1 $2
then
     rm $2
fi
```

**Table 1-2** *Understanding the* vacuum *shell script*

| The code ... | Uses ... | To ... |
|---|---|---|
| # shell script vacuum<br># This script finds...<br># Use it like this.<br># vacuum filename... | The pound sign ( # ) | Tell the shell that none of these lines are to be executed but that they are rather only commentary or internal documentation. |
| if cmp -s $1 $2 | ■ The keyword if to tell the shell that you want it to determine whether or not a specific condition exists<br>■ The command string cmp -s to tell the shell that this is what you want it to find out<br>■ The arguments $1 and $2 to tell the shell to run the command cmp on two filenames you're going to feed to it from the command line | Tell the shell to make a decision as to whether or not two files you name from the command line are the same. |

| The code . . . | Uses . . . | To . . . |
|---|---|---|
| then | The keyword that must accompany if | Tell the shell, "I'm about to give you instructions as to what you should do if the test I've asked you to carry out results in a true/yes/youbetcha answer." |
| rm $2 | ■ The command rm<br>■ The positional variable $2 | Tell the shell to get rid of the second file you named from the command line. |
| fi | Another keyword that must accompany if | Tell the shell you're done asking it to make decisions. |

### More complex if *statements in scripts*

As in life, not all decisions a shell script must make are as simple as the one we just examined. When a script needs to do different things, based on different sets of circumstances, one of the ways it can accomplish this is through an elaboration of the if structure, called if...else.

To illustrate if...else, we expand upon our script vacuum a bit and create a new script named hoover.

```
# shell script hoover
if cmp -s $1 $2
then
     rm $2
     echo Got rid of the duplicate file $2.
else
     echo We found no duplicates here.
fi
```

Now, in Table 1-3, we dissect hoover in the same way we did earlier with vacuum.

**Table 1-3** *Understanding the* hoover *shell script*

| The code . . . | Tells the shell . . . |
|---|---|
| `if cmp -s $1 $2` | Make a decision as to whether or not two files you name from the command line are the same. |
| `then` | "I'm about to give you instructions as to what you should do if the test I've asked you to carry out proves true." |
| `rm $2` | Get rid of the second file you named from the command line. |
| `echo Got rid of the duplicate file $2.` | Inform you when it's deleted the duplicate file. |
| `else` | You're about to give it instructions as to what to do if the test it's just run fails, that is, in this example, if the two files it's compared aren't the same. |
| `echo We found no duplicates here.` | You want these specific instructions carried out if the test fails. |
| `fi` | You're done asking it to make decisions. |

### Multiple branching with the case statement

In a way, the if...else structure we just digested, and more extensive examples of the use of this structure, offer programmers the means of selecting from a number of alternatives. But the more extensive the if structure, the more you'll begin to notice its shortcomings:

- You must, of course, type in all those lines.

- The shell must examine each one until one of them succeeds.

In other words, extensive if structures may not execute efficiently, especially when the shell must examine each and every alternative you've supplied.

A more sensible way to cause the shell to select from a number of alternatives is to use the case structure. Let's rewrite vacuum/hoover, to turn it into a script that

- offers you a menu

- cleans up files based on how you respond to that menu

```
# shell script menu_vac
echo Please enter the number which corresponds
echo to the task you have in mind.
echo '1 remove all files from the directory oldstuf'
echo '2 compare files in order to remove duplicates'
read entry
case $entry in
1) rm /oldstuf/*
```

```
   break
   ;;
2) if cmp -s $1 $2
   then
     rm $2
     echo Got rid of the duplicate file $2.
   Else

     echo We found no duplicates here.

   fi
   break
        ;;
esac
```

And now it's time to pull menu_vac apart, in Table 1-4.

**Table 1-4** *Understanding the* menu_vac *shell script*

| The code ... | Tells the shell ... |
|---|---|
| echo Please enter the number which corresponds | To present this text to you. |
| echo to the task you have in mind. | To present this text to you. |
| echo '1 remove all files from the directory oldstuf' | To present everything between the single quotes to you, on a new line. |
| echo ' compare files in order to remove duplicates' | Ditto. |
| read entry | Take whatever you enter at the keyboard, and place it in the entry variable. |
| case $entry in | You're about to give it instructions that pertain to the various possible values of entry. (The $ in front of the variable name means the shell must look at the contents of the variable.) |
| 1) rm /oldstuf/* | If the variable entry holds the value 1, indicating that you simply want to get rid of files, the shell should remove all files (*) in the indicated directory. |

*Continued*

**Table 1-4** *Continued*

| The code . . . | Tells the shell . . . |
|---|---|
| break | Don't look at any other options for possible values of the variable entry. |
| ;; | The processing of the case statement is finished. |
| 2) if cmp -s $1 $2<br>... etc ... | If the variable entry holds the value 2, indicating that you want to remove only duplicate files, the shell should carry out the code we originally wrote for vacuum and hoover. |
| break | Don't look at any other options for possible values of the variable entry. |
| ;; | The processing of the case statement is finished. |
| esac | You're done giving it a list of alternatives. |

# Looping

Like all programming environments, UNIX provides you with the ability to carry out the same instruction or set of instructions a number of times. That is, it lets you *loop*. But unlike true programming languages such as FORTRAN or Pascal, UNIX programming, at least UNIX shell script programming, is a bit loop-challenged; it gives you only two types of loops with which to work. The most widely used of these is the for loop.

### for *loops*

for loops cause the shell to repeat itself a specific number of times. Here's a small script that uses a for loop to express our long-term affection for all things Trek.

```
#script i_luv_trek
for x in spock data tuvok
do
     echo I love logical guys like $x
done
```

First, let's take a look at this script's output, shown in Figure 1-14.

```
#
# cat i_luv_trek

for x in spock data tuvok
do
  echo I love logical guys like $x
done
#
# i_luv_trek
I love logical guys like spock
I love logical guys like data
I love logical guys like tuvok
#
```

**Figure 1-14** *Can you guess that we're Star Trek fans?*

Now let's pull the script apart in Table 1-5.

**Table 1-5** *Understanding the* `i_luv_trek` *shell script*

| The line . . . | Tells the shell . . . |
|---|---|
| `for x in spock data tuvok` | For every supplied value of the variable x, that is, in this case, for each of the strings `spock`, `data`, and `tuvok`. |
| `do` | Carry out whatever I tell you next. |
| `echo I love logical guys like $x` | Which in this case is to display the phrase `I love logical guys like`, followed by the current value of the variable x. |
| `done` | You're done cycling through the repetitive set of operations. |

## while *loops*

`while` loops, on the other hand, set no quantitative limit on the number of times a loop will execute, or *iterate*, as more formal programming parlance calls it. Instead, `while` loops run until the condition that controls them is no longer true.

Suppose that we want to search a listing of files in the directory `trek_trivia` for all filenames that contain the string `trek`. Let's assume further that, as soon as we find a filename that does not hold this string, we want to display a message to that effect, and then end the script. Here's a shell script that will do both:

```
# script find_trek_files
while ls /trek_trivia/* | grep trek $1 > /dev/null
do
break
done

echo Just found a non-Trek file.
```

Now let's break this new script down with Table 1-6.

**Table 1-6** *Understanding the shell script* `find_trek_files`

| The line . . . | Tells the shell . . . |
|---|---|
| `while ls /trek_trivia/* | grep trek $1 > /dev/null` | As long as the `grep` command finds the string `trek` in the filenames produced by the `ls` command. |
| `do` | Here's what to do. |

*Continued*

**Table 1-6** *Continued*

| The line . . . | Tells the shell . . . |
|---|---|
| break | Jump out of the while loop. |
| done | You're done with the list of instructions as to what should happen if the test contained in the first line of the loop passes. |
| echo Just found a non-Trek file. | If the test contained in the first line of the loop fails, and the loop therefore no longer keeps running, this line will be executed. |

One last thing about the script find_trek_files. The phrase

```
$1 > /dev/null
```

tells the shell that, rather than displaying the actual results of the grep command's search for the string trek, it should simply discard them, shoving them into what old UNIX hands sometimes call the "bit bucket," a sort of black hole for unwanted data. Stuff goes in, but it never comes out; nothing can escape /dev/null.

## until *loops*

To some, until loops are no more than a variation on the while loop's theme. But many consider this type of loop a category unto itself. Where do we stand on the question? With one foot firmly planted on each side of the fence.

until loops are like mirror-image reflections of their while peers. In a while loop, as we've seen, as soon as the condition that controls the loop ceases to be true, so does the loop cease. With an until loop, on the other hand, the loop won't even begin to run if its test condition is already true, and will stop running the minute that condition becomes so.

Let's rewrite find_trek_files by way of illustration.

```
# script find_trek_files_2
until ls /trek_trivia/* | grep trek $1 > /dev/null
do
break
done
echo Just found a Trek file!
```

Now on to our usual dissection of the code, in Table 1-7.

Remember, an until loop starts running if a given condition is not yet met, and stops when that condition finally materializes. The while loop, on the other hand, won't even begin to execute if its control condition isn't satisfied.

*Hip Pocket Guide to UNIX*

**Table 1-7** *Understanding the shell script* `find_trek_files_2`

| The line . . . | Tells the shell . . . |
|---|---|
| `until ls /trek_trivia/* \|`<br>`grep trek $1 > /dev/null` | Until the `grep` command finds the string `trek` in the filenames produced by the `ls` command . . . |
| `do` | . . . here's what to do. |
| `break` | Jump out of the loop. |
| `done` | You're done with the list of instructions as to what should happen until the test contained in the first line of the loop passes . . . |
| `echo Just found a Trek file!` | . . . but when that test does finally succeed, the loop stops running, and this line will be executed. |

# Simple sample scripts

In this section we give you the complete code for a couple of shell scripts. One acts as a phone directory; the other is one of our personal favorites — a jargon generator.

## Keeping in touch

For a data file structured like this:

```
name1 phone-num1
```

which contains entries like these:

```
FuzzKatz    610-355-2405
L.B.Katz   302-358-2504
```

this shell script allows you to retrieve the complete phone number for a given individual.

```
#script phn_lst
#usage phn_lst name
grep $1 $HOME/phn_book
```

Note the use, in this script's final line, of the environment variable `HOME`, and its contents. By prefacing this value to the name of the script's input file, we ensure that only the copy of the file in our home directory, not some older or pirated version elsewhere in the file system, will be used by this script.

## Building buzz

We've come to one of our favorite scripts — a jargon generator, which, with slight modification, can be used to poke gentle fun at almost any field of endeavor.

```
#script buzz-builder
#The next three lines echo a carriage return.
```

```
#3 tabs, and the indicated message.
echo "\n\t\t\t\Welcome to the Buzzword Builder!"
echo "\n\t\t\t\Amaze your friends!"
echo "\n\t\t\t\Mystify your colleagues!"
#The next line, because it makes the empty command,
#that is, the :, the control
#for the while loop,
#causes that loop to keep running until the user
#presses the ENTER key.
while :
do
 echo "\nEnter a 2-digit number, or press ENTER to exit. \c"
echo "\n\t 0. Parallel      0. System"
echo "\n\t 1. Organizational 1. Platform"
echo "\n\t 2. Intermediate   2. Concept"
echo "\n\t 3. Digital        3. Suite"
echo "\n\t 4. Scalable       4. Engine"
echo "\n\t 5. Interactive    5. Driver"
echo "\n\t 6. Synchronized   6. Module"
echo "\n\t 7. Reciprocal     7. Component"
echo "\n\t 8. Iterative      8. Object"
echo "\n\t 9. Transitional   9. System"
 read numbr
#Here's where we test for the signal to exit.
 if test "$numbr" = ""
 then
  exit
 fi
#If the use has entered anything else,
#we cut that entry into 2 one-character columns.
#We've used grave accents, not single quotes, here
#to indicate that the result of the compound command
#they enclose are to be treated as a string.
 word1=`echo $numbr|cut -c1`
 word2=`echo $numbr|cut -c2`
#We start our buzz-phrase off as an empty string.
 buzz=""
#Then, depending upon the values we pulled out
#of the number our user entered,
#we assign suitable high-flown words to our buzz phrase.
 case $word1 in
  0)buzz="${buzz} Parallel ";;
  1)buzz="${buzz} Organizational ";;
```

```
2)buzz="${buzz} Intermediate ";;
3)buzz="${buzz} Digital ";;
4)buzz="${buzz} Scalable ";;
5)buzz="${buzz} Interactive ";;
6)buzz="${buzz} Synchronized ";;
7)buzz="${buzz} Reciprocal ";;
8)buzz="${buzz} Iterative ";;
9)buzz="${buzz} Transitional ";;
esac
case $word2 in
0)buzz="${buzz}System";;
1)buzz="${buzz}Platform ";;
2)buzz="${buzz}Concept";;
3)buzz="${buzz}Suite";;
4)buzz="${buzz}Engine";;
5)buzz="${buzz}Driver";;
6)buzz="${buzz}Module";;
7)buzz="${buzz}Component";;
8)buzz="${buzz}Object";;
9)buzz="${buzz}Paradigm";;
esac
echo "\n You have created the soon-to-be-hot buzz "$buzz"
done
```

# The UNIX File System

As this book was being written, we heard a news item regarding a new development in hard disk storage. IBM Corporation announced that it had succeeded in creating a disk that stored hundreds of gigabits per square inch of a disk's surface. When you consider that the useful surface area of an average hard drive is at least a dozen square inches, you begin to appreciate the storage potential this entails.

What does this have to do with UNIX file systems? IBM's announcement is one more bit of evidence of something we've all come to assume — that computer hardware will continue to evolve in the direction of greater capacity and power. The UNIX file system is ideally suited to managing the kinds of storage in drives like those being developed by IBM.

## Byte sequences

At its simplest, a UNIX file system is no more than a huge collection of bytes. The system imposes no limitations on the nature of the data that can be placed in individual files. Binary, ASCII, WordPerfect — you name it — UNIX will accept files with any internal formatting you like. It's how UNIX organizes the data it stores and manages, not the internal format of that data, that's important. A UNIX file system can be pictured as a tree capable of a nearly infinite number of branches, each of which in turn can sprout any number of leaves. While Figure 1-15 doesn't have room to show more than a very few of these branches, we think it will help you understand the organization of a UNIX file system.

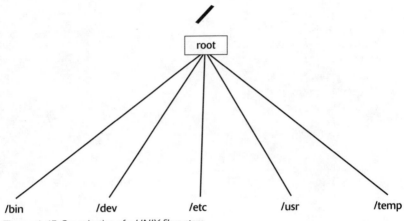

**Figure 1-15** *Organization of a UNIX file system*

## A hierarchy

All this, of course, shares a single root or base. Such a file system, organized as an inverted tree structure and used not only by UNIX but also by a number of other operating systems, is known in technical terms as a *hierarchy*.

In a hierarchical file system such as that used by UNIX, only files actually contain the data you'd expect. Directories and subdirectories don't themselves hold files. Rather, they maintain pointers to where the files are located. In strictest UNIX parlance, a directory is itself a file that contains file location information called *inodes*. In managing directories, that is, in maintaining information on inodes, UNIX uses another system-level file called the *superblock*. The superblock is again a file, but one which tracks all inode tables on a UNIX machine in the same way an inode table tracks files in a directory.

At the root of a UNIX file system is the root directory, always indicated by a forward slash ( / ). From this entry-point into a UNIX file system, a number of standard directories branch, which we've outlined in Table 1-8. While a system administrator can vary the amount of storage each of these directories can use, their function is so important to UNIX that the administrator would be ill-advised, or even unable, to omit them from a UNIX system's configuration.

**Table 1-8** *Standard UNIX directories*

| This area of a UNIX file system . . . | Whose name stands for . . . | Typically houses . . . |
| --- | --- | --- |
| /bin | Binary | Commonly used UNIX commands or binaries |
| /dev | Devices | Information on every piece of hardware that makes up the system |
| /etc | Et cetera | Miscellaneous or hard-to-categorize items; includes the password file |
| /tmp | Temporary | Throwaway stuff |
| /usr | User | User directories and files |

# Device independence

Under UNIX, every physical device that helps make up a computer, and in some cases, a section of such a device, is handled as if it were simply a file. And we do mean *every*. Even such physical resources as memory and areas of a hard drive have, under UNIX, a file persona.

So you, as a user of UNIX, can produce hard copy output by redirecting the results of, let's say, the cat command to the file /dev/lp. Or, you could, if you were feeling really adventurous, change a single byte in memory by changing the contents of /dev/mem.

The life of a UNIX system programmer isn't quite this laid-back, though. Such folks must write device drivers, programs that control the functioning of everything from modems to printers to CD-ROM drives, in order to control the operations of those devices, and to allow them to communicate with the kernel. Such programs, called special files because UNIX uses them to access and control hardware, have their own place in the file system. After being compiled, they become, at least under many versions of UNIX, part of the path /unix. In every flavor of UNIX, though, they're part of the executable code that makes up the OS once they're compiled.

It's the way in which conversations between UNIX and the devices they control take place that determines the further characterization of device drivers. Those which deal with devices — modems, terminals, or printers — which in turn deal with data as a character-by-character stream are referred to as *character-special files*. Those, on the other hand, which handle resources like disk drives, which organize data into blocks, are known as *block-special files*.

In either case, this scheme of representing physical devices, and their communication with the operating system, as files, allows UNIX to be largely device-independent. Drivers for a wide variety of components are compiled right into the

OS. And if there proves to be a need for more or new drivers, the solution is simple. Install the programs, recompile the kernel, reboot your UNIX system, and you're back in business.

## Mounting and unmounting file systems

While UNIX knows about any and all devices with which it must converse from the get-go, or at least from the time it was most recently recompiled, it doesn't necessarily have every aspect of every file system associated with such devices immediately in mind.

Even the physically simplest UNIX file system may rely on a hard drive that's been partitioned into several sections. Only the root file system, those directories — usually the most essential — that branch directly from /, are automatically made available when a UNIX machine is booted. Others, such as those that reside on a CD-ROM drive or a diskette drive, can remain hidden from the OS's attention even though it is aware of the devices associated with such file systems. In order to be able to work with collections of files like these, you must mount the file system involved. That is, you must explicitly tell UNIX, "Associate this file system with the device file I indicate."

So, if you want to work with files on a floppy, for instance, you must issue the command

```
mount /dev/fd0 /floppy
```

or, on some UNIX machines

```
/etc/mount /dev/fd0 /floppy
```

When that's done, you can work with the files in the system /floppy in the same way you'd deal with those in root ( / ), or in any of its subsystems, such as /usr, /bin, /dev, or /etc.

And when *that's* done, if you want to ensure the integrity of the files in the /floppy system, you can unmount that system with this command:

```
umount /floppy
```

Note that when dissolving a file system/UNIX partnership, you don't need to specify the physical device with which the system has been associated. UNIX has remembered that.

Aside from allowing you to create or get rid of operating system/file system duos, UNIX's scheme of mounting and unmounting file systems has another, less obvious advantage. It allows you to find out which file groups are associated with particular storage devices at any given moment. So, keying in

```
/etc/mount
```

all by itself at the command prompt might produce a result like that shown in Figure 1-16.

```
#
#
# /etc/mount
/ on /dev/vg00/lvol3 defaults on Wed Nov  5 11:01:06 1997
/stand on /dev/vg00/lvol1 defaults on Wed Nov  5 11:01:08 1997
/var on /dev/vg00/lvol8 defaults on Wed Nov  5 11:01:18 1997
/usr on /dev/vg00/lvol7 defaults on Wed Nov  5 11:01:19 1997
/tmp on /dev/vg00/lvol6 defaults on Wed Nov  5 11:01:19 1997
/opt on /dev/vg00/lvol5 defaults on Wed Nov  5 11:01:19 1997
/home on /dev/vg00/lvol4 defaults on Wed Nov  5 11:01:19 1997
/backup on /dev/vg00/backup defaults on Wed Nov  5 11:01:19 1997
#
```

**Figure 1-16** *As you can see, there were eight file systems mounted when we snapped this shot.*

This display tells us, among other things, that

- the file system var is affiliated with the device known as /dev/vg00/lvol8, a hard disk partition.

- the file system tmp is affiliated with the device known as /dev/vg00/lvol6, a hard disk partition.

- the file system home is affiliated with the device known as /dev/vg00/lvol4, a hard disk partition.

These file systems, because they branch directly from the root and because they reside on devices that have been compiled into the OS, will never be unmounted.

# File security

Historically, UNIX has earned a bad rap as far as its attention to security goes. When you recall that the OS was designed to be open and flexible, there might at first seem to be some basis in fact for this charge. But while it's true that UNIX has no means of password protecting individual files or directories, it has a security system just as powerful, if not more so.

The actions that individual users, be they a file's owner, members of the user group to which the owner belongs, or anybody else, may take in working with a file can be closely configured, as Figure 1-17 illustrates. Those actions include the ability to

- read, that is look at, the file

- write to, which also means copy or delete, the file

- if appropriate, execute the file

What's more, you can tailor these three levels of access for each of these three user categories for every file and directory on a UNIX system.

```
# ls -l|more
total 106
-rw-r--r--   1 daemon    daemon      2326 Jul 18 17:42 apache_pb.gif
-rw-r-----   1 daemon    daemon      2998 Dec 11 13:14 books1a.gif
-rw-r-----   1 daemon    daemon      2899 Dec 11 13:14 books2a.gif
-rw-r--r--   1 daemon    daemon      2899 Dec  2 12:19 bookshlf.gif
-rw-rw-rw-   1 root      sys           48 Dec 17 18:41 cutout
-rw-rw-rw-   1 root      sys            2 Dec 17 18:28 hobo00
-rw-rw-rw-   1 root      sys          127 Dec 17 18:28 hobo01
-rw-rw-rw-   1 root      sys          272 Dec 17 18:57 howdif
-rw-r--r--   1 daemon    daemon      1908 Nov 21 17:18 hz_dccclib.gif
-rw-r-----   1 daemon    daemon      2222 Dec 19 12:54 index.html
-rw-r--r--   1 daemon    daemon       668 Dec 11 13:28 index.html.most.rec
-rw-r--r--   1 daemon    daemon      1316 Nov 21 16:26 index.html.orig
-rw-r--r--   1 daemon    daemon       754 Nov 26 10:15 index.html.two
-rw-rw-rw-   1 root      sys        13340 Dec 17 16:45 kungfu
-rwx------   1 root      sys           66 Dec 17 17:12 look4chan
drwxrwxrwx   5 daemon    daemon      1024 Nov  5 11:48 manual
-rw-rw-rw-   1 root      sys           23 Dec 17 17:10 new.htm
-rw-rw-rw-   1 root      sys           21 Dec 17 19:46 ok_triv
-rw-rw-rw-   1 root      sys           25 Dec 17 17:36 savemail
-rw-rw-rw-   1 root      sys           25 Dec 17 18:45 somefile
-rw-rw-rw-   1 root      sys           25 Dec 17 18:49 someotherfile
-rw-rw-rw-   1 root      sys          129 Dec 17 18:18 specialmsgs
Standard input
```

**Figure 1-17** *Notice the variety of permissions associated with these files and directories.*

Table 1-9 translates the file access modes available under UNIX to both literal and numeric representations.

**Table 1-9** *Understanding UNIX file access permissions*

| Access mode . . . | Represented as . . . | Binary notation | Translates as . . . | Arrived at by . . . |
|---|---|---|---|---|
| read | r | 0 if unavailable, 1 if present | Remember, each of the octal digits in an access permission represents three binary digits. | |
| write | w | 0 if unavailable, 1 if present | | |
| execute | x | 0 if unavailable, 1 if present | ■ For read access only, 4 <br> ■ For write access only, 2 <br> ■ For execute access only, 1 <br> ■ For read and write access, 6 <br> ■ For read and execute access, 5 <br> ■ For write and execute access, 3 <br> ■ For read, write, and execute access, 7 | ■ Translating the binary notation 100, whose columns when read left to right represent a 4, a 2, and a 1 respectively <br> ■ Translating the binary notation 010 <br> ■ Translating the binary notation 001 <br> ■ Translating the binary notation 110 |

| Access mode . . . | Represented as . . . | Binary notation | Translates as . . . | Arrived at by . . . |
|---|---|---|---|---|
| | | | | ■ Translating the binary notation 101<br>■ Translating the binary notation 011<br>■ Translating the binary notation 111 |

Now let's put our calculators aside, and review the UNIX file access permissions you can build with this scheme. Note that Table 1-10 assumes that a file's owner would always have all of read, write, and execute capabilities. In the real world, of course, this need not be the case. Like anyone else, a file's owner can be assigned, or can assign himself or herself, any combination of file access permissions. So, at least in theory, nothing prevents a 6, 5, 4, or 3 from occupying that first column in an overall file access permission.

**Table 1-10** *Breaking down UNIX file access permissions*

| An overall file access permission of . . . | Assigns, to a file's owner . . . | To members of the owner's group . . . | And to everyone else . . . |
|---|---|---|---|
| 777 | Read, write, and execute (octal 7 = binary 111) | Read, write, and execute (octal 7 = binary 111) | Read, write, and execute (octal 7 = binary 111) |
| 776 | Read, write, and execute (octal 7 = binary 111) | Read, write, and execute (octal 7 – binary 111) | Read and write (octal 6 = binary 110) |
| 766 | Read, write, and execute (octal 7 = binary 111) | Read and write (octal 6 = binary 110) | Read and write (octal 6 = binary 110) |
| 765 | Read, write, and execute (octal 7 = binary 111) | Read and write (octal 6 = binary 110) | Read and execute (octal 5 = binary 101) |
| 755 | Read, write, and execute (octal 7 = binary 111) | Read and execute (octal 5 = binary 101) | Read and execute (octal 5 = binary 101) |
| 754 | Read, write, and execute (octal 7 = binary 111) | Read and execute (octal 5 = binary 101) | Only read (octal 4 = binary 100) |

*Continued*

**Table 1-10** *Continued*

| An overall file access permission of . . . | Assigns, to a file's owner . . . | To members of the owner's group . . . | And to everyone else . . . |
|---|---|---|---|
| 744 | Read, write, and execute (octal 7 = binary 111) | Only read (octal 4 = binary 100) | Only read (octal 4 = binary 100) |
| 743 | Read, write, and execute (octal 7 = binary 111) | Only read (octal 4 = binary 100) | Write and execute (octal 3 = binary 011) |
| 733 | Read, write, and execute (octal 7 = binary 111) | Write and execute (octal 3 = binary 011) | Write and execute (octal 3 = binary 011) |

Let's recap what you've learned so far. You've discovered the nature and flavors of UNIX, looked at its command lines in a number of their possible forms, examined the shell as a programming environment and even written a few shell scripts, and finally investigated UNIX file access permissions. In the next section, we scrutinize nearly one hundred UNIX commands, and present not only their general syntax but examples of using them.

# UNIX COMMANDS

This section presents nearly 100 UNIX commands and gives you the following information for each of them:

- The name of the command
- A brief description of what the command does
- A generic look at the command's syntax
- A real-world example of how to use the command
- A bit more discussion of the command's nature and behavior

# ar

## FUNCTION

ar creates and manages file archives and archive libraries. Under UNIX, an *archive* is a collection of files that have been condensed and combined to make a single file.

## GENERAL SYNTAX

```
ar archive-key [ordinal] archive [list]
```

| The parameter . . . | Indicates . . . |
| --- | --- |
| archive-key | The string is needed to access the archive. It can be any of d, r, q, t, p, and more, which indicate respectively deleting named files from an archive; replacing named files within an archive; quickly appending named files to the end of an archive; showing a table of contents for the archive; and displaying the actual contents of the files in the archive. |
| ordinal | The position within the archive of a file; usually indicated by the file's name. |
| archive | The name of the archive file itself. |
| list | The list of files to be incorporated into the archive. |

## SNEAK PREVIEW

```
# ar q kungfu *.gif
ar: creating kungfu
#
#
# ar t kungfu
apache_pb.gif
books1a.gif
books2a.gif
bookshlf.gif
hz_dcoclib.gif
```

## DESCRIPTION

As you can see from the Sneak Preview, entering **ar t kungfu** produces a listing of all files in the archive of that name. (Of course, we first had to create the archive.)

## RELATED COMMANDS

cpio, tar

# awk

## FUNCTION

awk is a mini-programming language that excels at text processing. Those of you familiar with BASIC will feel right at home with awk.

## GENERAL SYNTAX

```
awk [-F field delimiter] script file [additional parameters] [data
input file]
```

| The parameter . . . | Indicates . . . |
|---|---|
| -F field delimiter | A character, other than the default space (ASCII 32), that you wish awk to separate into fields to be processed. |
| script file | The name of the file that contains the awk program you want to run. |
| additional parameters | Such things as the creation and initialization of a variable. |
| data input file | If input for your awk program doesn't come from standard input (the keyboard), then this file holds the data your program will process. |

## SNEAK PREVIEW

```
# cat look4chan
{if ($1=="JackieChan") printf "Found one in file %s\n", FILENAME}
#
#
# cat new.htm
JackieChan
JackieChan

#
# awk -f look4chan *.htm
Found one in file new.htm
Found one in file new.htm
```

## DESCRIPTION

Let's suppose you're doing research for the creation of a Web page about one of your favorite subjects, Jackie Chan movies. Rather than read all your source material, you could write a small awk program, or run an awk command from the operating system prompt that would search through all these source files and locate every line that had the phrase *Jackie Chan* at the beginning of the line.

```
awk -f look4chan *.htm
```

The awk program look4chan contains these lines:

```
{if ("$1 $2" == "JackieChan" printf "Found in ", "%s\n", FILENAME}
```

## RELATED COMMANDS

sh, vi

---

# banner

## FUNCTION

banner displays any string supplied to it as a parameter in large characters.

## GENERAL SYNTAX

    banner [string]

| The parameter . . . | Indicates . . . |
|---|---|
| string | The words or message will be output in outsized characters. |

## SNEAK PREVIEW

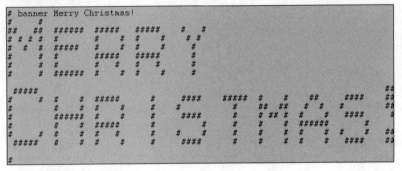

## DESCRIPTION

banner is one of those fun UNIX commands that tests your creativity. You may create an impromptu birthday poster on the fly. Or, you may indulge your imagination and produce all manner of messages, silly and otherwise. Just remember, any character you enter from the keypad will be as large as the creatures in *Jurassic Park*.

---

# basename

## FUNCTION

basename strips away all but the innermost level of any path name you give it as an argument.

## GENERAL SYNTAX

basename *string*

| The parameter . . . | Indicates . . . |
|---|---|
| string | A directory path in a file system; for example, /usr/bin |

## SNEAK PREVIEW

```
#
# basename /usr/bin
bin
#
```

## DESCRIPTION

basename is straightforward. If, for any reason, you want the innermost level of a path name returned, type something like:

basename /usr/bin

UNIX and basename will respond by telling you that the innermost level of this path is bin.

## RELATED COMMANDS

dirname

# batch

## FUNCTION

`batch` runs tasks when the operating system has time, that is, as a batch job at the OS's discretion rather than at a time specified by the user.

## GENERAL SYNTAX

```
batch task [list] <Ctrl-D>
```

| The parameter . . . | Indicates . . . |
|---|---|
| `task [list]` | The command or task list that the system is to execute |
| `Ctrl-D` | The end of the command or task list to be executed |

## SNEAK PREVIEW

```
# batch lst4book
warning: commands will be executed using /usr/bin/sh
job 884465877.b at Sat Jan 10 15:57:57 1998
#
```

## DESCRIPTION

`batch` is a command that appears to have taken its profile from one of its UNIX relatives called `cron`. Although you learn about `cron` later, a quick look at the similarities and contrasts between the two can only help reinforce your understanding. Both commands run tasks or list of tasks on the operating system. And you set `batch` in motion by pressing Ctrl+D. `batch`, however, differs from `cron` in two important ways.

First, `batch` can be executed from either the command line or a file. If you run it from the command line but supply no arguments, it will even prompt you for them, whereas `cron` must use a special file called `crontab`, in which the dates and times to run certain jobs are indicated. The presence of those dates and times in `crontab` is the second important distinction between `batch` and `cron`. The `cron` command runs things on a repeating schedule. `batch` only runs its tasks when the system has time, and even then only once.

You may think of `batch` as a kind of poor man's `cron`. It's nothing fancy. However, when it's time to go home and you still need to run that certain job sometime today, think of `batch`.

## RELATED COMMANDS

`at`, `cron`

# cal

## FUNCTION
cal displays a calendar for a month or a year.

## GENERAL SYNTAX
    cal [month] [year]

| The parameter ... | Indicates ... |
|---|---|
| month | Any month from 1 through 12 |
| year | Any year from 1 to 9999 A.D. |

## SNEAK PREVIEW

```
#
# cal 10 1997
    October 1997
 S  M Tu  W Th  F  S
             1  2  3  4
 5  6  7  8  9 10 11
12 13 14 15 16 17 18
19 20 21 22 23 24 25
26 27 28 29 30 31
#
```

## DESCRIPTION
To show the calendar for October, 1999, type **cal 10 1999** and press Enter.
For the Trekkers among you, we're sorry to say that cal doesn't display stardates.

## RELATED COMMANDS
date

# cancel

## FUNCTION

cancel provides for the cancellation of a printing request initiated with lp, a line printer command.

## GENERAL SYNTAX

    cancel [id(s)] [printer(s)]

| The parameter . . . | Indicates . . . |
|---|---|
| id(s) | The ID number of the printing task. The number is actually created by the lp (or print) command. Find the ID number to cancel a print task by using the line printer status command lpstat. |
| printer(s) | You want to cancel the task from this printer. |

## SNEAK PREVIEW

```
#
# cancel 127
```

## DESCRIPTION

cancel is a command with a lot of interplay from its buddies, lp and lpstat. Other things need to happen before you use cancel. First you need to have requested the printing of a file using lp.

As soon as you accomplish the above, you have already won the ID number. And cancel has the key to do its magic. Once you enter cancel together with the necessary ID, the deed is done.

You should know one last thing: under some flavors of UNIX, cancel either doesn't exist, as in Linux, or is replaced by the command called lprm (for *line printer remove*), as in Berkeley UNIX. In addition, both of these operating systems substitute lpr for lp, and lpq for lpstat.

## RELATED COMMANDS

lp, lpstat

# cat

## FUNCTION

cat allows you either to look at files or join them together.

## GENERAL SYNTAX

```
cat file1 [>] [file2]
```

| The parameter... | Indicates... |
|---|---|
| file1 | cat will display this file's contents. |
| > | The contents of file1 are to be appended to the contents of file2. |
| file2 | This file's contents will be appended by file1. |

## SNEAK PREVIEW

```
#
# cat savemail

No new mail so far.

# cat specialmsgs

Nothing here either.

# cat savemail >> specialmsgs
#
# cat specialmsgs

Nothing here either.



No new mail so far.
```

## DESCRIPTION

The cat command is short for concatenate. Using cat to look at a file would go as follows:

```
cat savemail
```

Then you would press Enter.

This entry would cause UNIX to display the entire contents of the file savemail on your screen (even if the file is too long to fit on a single screen). Using cat to join two files would be done in this way:

```
cat savemail > specialmsgs
```

Then, press Enter.

Typing the string above would *append* the contents of the file `savemail` to those of the file `specialmsgs`. An important distinction is made by UNIX between >> and simply >. Both of these accomplish what the system knows as *redirection*, sending output to someplace other than where it would normally go. But >> appends, while > overwrites, destroying whatever else might have been there first.

**RELATED COMMANDS**

head, more, pg, tail

# CC

## FUNCTION

cc, while not part of UNIX (strictly speaking), is so closely related to it that we can't imagine a UNIX environment in which you won't find it. cc is the command you must use to compile a C program.

## GENERAL SYNTAX

```
cc [-c] [-o output file name] input file
```

| The parameter . . . | Indicates . . . |
|---|---|
| -c | The compiler should forego linking, and produce an object file. Be careful that you don't use c, or that you do so in combination with -o, if your source includes such standard C libraries as stdio or math. Otherwise you won't link in these libraries. |
| -o output file name | The compiler should name the executable it produces with the same name as the source file. |
| input file | You want to compile this C program. Make sure this source filename has the extension .c, or many compilers won't recognize the file. |

## SNEAK PREVIEW

```
#
# cat hithere.c
main()
printf ("Hi there, everybody!\n");
# cc -c hithere.c -ohithere
#
# ls a.out
a.out not found
# ls hithere
hithere
#
```

## DESCRIPTION

Entering the command cc hithere.c produces an output file arbitrarily named a.out. If you want to name your executable to match your source file, you must use the -o option. This is because cc actually kickstarts three processes, in this order: preprocessing, which resolves preprocessor directives such as #include; actual compilation; and linking in any needed library functions.

Another popular C language compiler on some UNIX systems is the Gnu C Compiler, which is started with the command gcc.

## RELATED COMMANDS

make

---

# cd

## FUNCTION
cd changes the active directory to the one in which you wish to work.

## GENERAL SYNTAX
    cd [directory]

| The parameter . . . | Indicates . . . |
|---|---|
| directory | The name of the directory or directory path |

## SNEAK PREVIEW
```
#
# pwd
/usr/bin
#
# cd /home/httpd
#
# pwd
/home/httpd
#
```

## DESCRIPTION
cd, like so many UNIX commands, is an acronym. Using cd allows you to change
directories, that is, move from working in one directory to working in another.

For example, the administrator's directory on a new library server is / or root. If,
for whatever reason, this administrator needed to look at a file in one of his machine's
Web server-related directories, he might enter:

    cd /home/httpd

Note how the forward slashes, starting with root (/), indicate moving down the
path through the server's file and directory structure.

## RELATED COMMANDS
ls, pwd

# chgrp

## FUNCTION

chgrp changes the affiliation of a file from one group ID to another. It is analogous to, but not precisely the same as, chown.

## GENERAL SYNTAX

    chgrp group file(s)

| The parameter . . . | Indicates . . . |
| --- | --- |
| group | The ID number which in turn indicates the group with which you want to associate a file or files |
| file(s) | The file or files you want to affiliate with the group |

## SNEAK PREVIEW

```
#
# ls -l 1st4book
-rw-rw-rw-   1 root        sys          3026 Jan 10 14:21 1st4book
# chgrp bin 1st4book
# ls -l 1st4book
-rw-rw-rw-   1 root        bin          3026 Jan 10 14:21 1st4book
#
```

## DESCRIPTION

In a way similar to chown, chgrp assigns possession or control of a file or files, not to an individual, but to a group. Take another look at the Sneak Preview. The output of the ls command, which you learn about in more detail later, shown there indicates that the group affiliation of the file we're working with has changed from sys to bin.

## RELATED COMMANDS

chmod, chown, ls

---

# chmod

## FUNCTION

chmod allows you to change the access mode associated with a file, tailoring access permissions for the file's owner, affiliated group, and all other users. So, file access permissions as manipulated by chmod are commonly referred to as *owner-group-world*.

## GENERAL SYNTAX

chmod numeric or alphabetic representation file name(s)

| The parameter . . . | Indicates . . . |
|---|---|
| numeric representation | With an octal number, what each of owner, group, and world can do with a file. In order to understand these octal representations, you must translate them into their binary equivalents. |
| alphabetic representation | The literal indication, by means of an r for *read*, a w for *write*, and an x for *execute*, of what each of owner, group, and world can do with a file. |
| file name | The name of the file for which to change permissions. |

## SNEAK PREVIEW

```
$ ls -l 1st4book
-rw-rw-rw-   1 root       sys         3026 Jan 10 14:21 1st4book
$ chgrp bin 1st4book
$ ls -l 1st4book
-rw-rw-rw-   1 root       bin         3026 Jan 10 14:21 1st4book
$ chmod 700 1st4book
$ ls -l 1st4book
-rwx------   1 root       bin         3026 Jan 10 14:21 1st4book
$
```

## DESCRIPTION

Let's say you want to make the file kungfu.htm read-only for the majority of users, read/write for members of the group chanfan, and read/write/execute for you, the owner of the file. In other words, most users would be able to look at this file, but do no more. Members of the chanfan group, on the other hand, would be able not only to view but also to modify or even delete the file. You, as owner of the file, could do both these, and execute the file.

chmod gives you two ways to represent these file operations. If you use numeric representation and wish to indicate the variety of access we just described, you would type **chmod 764 kungfu.htm**.

In this command line, the individual digits translate as indicated in the table below.

| chmod "column" ... | Represents ... | Translates to binary as ... | Which translates to decimal as ... |
|---|---|---|---|
| leftmost (7) | What a file's owner may do with the file. | 111, meaning ■ Yes, you can read the file. ■ Yes, you can edit, copy, or delete the file. ■ Yes, you can execute the file. (As is usually the case when using binary notation to denote true or false, chmod means true or yes when it uses a *1*, and no or false when it uses a *0*.) | 7 (1 + 2 + 4 = 7) |
| middle (6) | What a file's affiliated group may do with the file. | 110, meaning ■ Yes, you can read the file. ■ Yes, you can edit, copy, or delete the file. ■ No, you cannot execute the file. | 6 (0 + 2 + 4 = 6) |
| rightmost (4) | What all other users may do with the file. | 100, meaning ■ Yes, you can read the file. ■ No, you cannot edit, copy, or delete the file. ■ No, you cannot execute the file. | 4 (0 + 0 + 4 = 4) |

If you use alphabetic representation, and wish to indicate the access types we just described, you'd also have to use a plus (+) or a minus (-) sign, to indicate adding or removing particular permissions. For example, if you wished to add write permission for the file `kungfu.htm` for users other than the file's owner or group, you'd type **chmod o+w kungfu.htm**.

What this command tells UNIX is, "Let all users other than (o), the file's owner and affiliated group, be able to write (*w* — modify, copy, or delete) `kungfu.htm`."

**RELATED COMMANDS**

`chgrp`, `chown`, `ls`

# chown

## FUNCTION

chown , which stands for *change owner,* changes the ownership of a file.

## GENERAL SYNTAX

    chown owner file

| The parameter . . . | Indicates . . . |
|---|---|
| owner | This is the user to whom you wish to give ownership of the file. |
| file | An individual owns this file after the command is executed. |

## SNEAK PREVIEW

```
#
# pwd
/home
# ls -l lb_fil
-rw-rw-rw-    1 bin        bin          34 Feb  6 17:01 lb_fil
# chown fuzz lb_fil
# ls -l lb_fil
-rw-rw-rw-    1 bin        bin          34 Feb  6 17:01 lb_fil
#
```

## DESCRIPTION

If I enter:

    chown fuzz lb_fil

and my UNIX system has an entry in its file /etc/passwd for a user named fuzz, then the user (fuzz) now has control over the file lb_fil. This means fuzz can change the read-write-execute permissions having to do with this file. fuzz can also chown the file to someone else. Note, too, that when we examine permissions for the file, as in the Sneak Preview, the group to which both lb and fuzz belong is listed as the owner of the file. That's a quirk of the version of UNIX under which we tested these commands, and of the way in which the particular machine on which we tested them was configured. In most cases, after running chown, the user to whom ownership of the file had been changed would show in a listing of the file as the owner. And one more thing: many UNIX systems are configured to allow only the superuser root to chown files; this is done as a security measure, to deny hackers the opportunity to write a program that does bad things such as change its ownership to root, and then make use of root's extraordinary powers to do awful stuff.

## RELATED COMMANDS

chgrp, chmod, ls

# clear

**FUNCTION**

clear clears your monitor and places the cursor at the upper-left corner of the newly blank screen.

**GENERAL SYNTAX**

```
clear
```

**SNEAK PREVIEW / DESCRIPTION**

We do not include a figure here for two reasons. First, clear is self-explanatory. And second, since the physical size and the definition of monitors' UNIX screen capacity varies from system to system, clear may not always remove everything from your display. For instance, when we connect to one of the UNIX servers we've used to test the commands and take the figures in this book, the display size of our PC's monitor matches that defined for terminals of the server, and clear does just fine. But on our other UNIX test machine, we consistently end up with three lines still straggling along at the top of the display, even after we've run clear.

# cmp

## FUNCTION
cmp allows you to compare the contents of any two files.

## GENERAL SYNTAX
    cmp [-l] [-s] file1 file2

| The parameter . . . | Indicates . . . |
|---|---|
| -l | The positions of the differing bytes in the files are displayed in decimal. The bytes themselves are presented in octal — go figure. |
| -s | Differing files produce no output except a return of codes, which indicate the condition they were in when they stopped running. |
| file1 | This file will be compared against file2 for differences in content. |
| file2 | This file will be compared against file1 for differences in content. |

## SNEAK PREVIEW
```
#
# cat tom1
xxxxxxxxxxxxcxxx
#
# cat tom2
xxxxxxxxxxxxCxxx
#
# cmp tom1 tom2
tom1 tom2 differ: char 13, line 1
#
# cmp -l tom1 tom2
    13 143 103
#
```

## DESCRIPTION
Say you want to compare the contents of two files, tom1 and tom2. If you use the command cmp tom1 tom2 to compare the files tom1 and tom2, you'll get the following result:

    tom1 tom2 differ: char 13, line1

which tells us that the content of these two files begins to diverge at their mutual thirteenth character on line 1 in each file.

Try using -l to see what other parameters do. You'll see

- in column 1, the decimal positioning of the differing bytes in both files
- in column 2, the errant byte in octal from file1
- in column 3, the errant byte in octal from file2

## RELATED COMMANDS
comm, diff, dircmp

---

*Hip Pocket Guide to UNIX*

# comm

## FUNCTION
comm examines two sorted text files for similar or common lines.

## GENERAL SYNTAX
```
comm [-1 -2 -3] file1 file2
```

| The parameter . . . | Indicates . . . |
|---|---|
| -1 | Column 1, which is not to be displayed |
| -2 | Column 2, which is not to be displayed |
| -3 | Column 3, which is not to be displayed |
| file1 | The first sorted text file to be compared against file2 |
| file2 | The second sorted text file to be compared against file1 |

## SNEAK PREVIEW
```
#
# cat testdi
# cat testdigg
This is a test file.
This is not a test file.
This is another line.
This is another line.
This is not another duplicate line.

# cat testdigh
This is a test file.
This is not a test file.
This is another line.
This is not another duplicate line.

# comm -1 testdigg testdigh
        This is a test file.
        This is not a test file.
        This is another line.
        This is not another duplicate line.
#
```

## DESCRIPTION
comm uses the sort command to ready the files it wants to compare. Typing **sort -o file1 file1** sorts your text file alphabetically, taking the sorted output and writing it permanently back to file1. Do the same procedure on file2.

comm now compares the two previously sorted text files for three different "conditions," which it then displays in three different columns. Column 1 presents lines you'll only see in file1. Column 2 shows you lines you only find in file2. Column 3 shows lines common to both files.

## RELATED COMMANDS
cmp, diff, dircmp

---

# cp

## FUNCTION
cp makes a carbon copy of one file's contents and places those contents in another file.

## GENERAL SYNTAX
```
cp file1 file2
```

| The parameter . . . | Indicates . . . |
|---|---|
| file1 | You're going to copy this file's contents. |
| file2 | This file will receive the copy of the contents of file1. |

## SNEAK PREVIEW
```
#
# ls -l newtom
newtom not found
#
# cp tom1 newtom
#
# ls -l newtom
-r-xr-xr-x   1 root        sys            17 Dec 17 18:02 newtom
#
```

## DESCRIPTION
cp is a simple and useful command that will give you no trouble if you remember one thing: if you do not have permission to write a file, the copy will fail.

Assuming your permissions allow you write access to the file you want to copy, you can create a file on the fly by copying an old file's contents to a new filename. Furthermore, you can cp a file's contents to another file of the same name. But, that same-name destination file must be in another directory.

## RELATED COMMANDS
mv, del, ls

# cpio

## FUNCTION
cpio, like tar and ar, creates and manages file archives and archive libraries.

## GENERAL SYNTAX
    cpio -mode [options] [patterns] directory name

| The parameter . . . | Indicates . . . |
|---|---|
| mode | One of the following:<br>o (out) — Copies a list of files into an archive file<br>i (n) — Extracts individual files from an archive file<br>p (pass) — Copies files from one directory to another, without creating an archive file |
| options | For copy-out mode, includes the following:<br>a — Resets access times<br>c — Writes administrative information in text form<br>B — Uses a block size of 5,120 bytes for input and output<br>v — Verbose reports, or displays the name of every file processed<br>For copy-in mode, includes all the above except a, plus the following:<br>d — Creates directories as needed<br>m — Retains original file modification times<br>r — Renames files based upon values supplied by the user<br>t — Gives a table of contents of the archive file<br>u — Copies unconditionally, that is, replaces existing files with older versions from an archive<br>f — Copies all files *except* those named in the patterns argument<br>S or s — Swaps nibbles, that is, half-word or units of 4 bytes, within 8-byte words<br>b — Swaps individual bytes within half-words<br>For pass mode, includes a, d, l, m, u, and v, with l indicating linking files rather than copying them |
| patterns | The name or names of files that will *not* be copied |
| directory name | In pass mode, the destination directory |

## SNEAK PREVIEW

```
#
# ls *tom* | cpio -ov > onebigfile
bigtom
newtom
tom1
tom2
1 blocks
#
#
```

**DESCRIPTION**

The internal format used by `cpio` isn't compatible with that used by either `tar` or `ar`. In addition, also unlike `tar`, `cpio` does not block out space on a destination storage medium. This means that under `tar`, even a 5-byte file would take up an entire block of storage, be it 512 or 1,024 bytes, while under `cpio`, the 5-byte file would take up only 5 bytes (if your storage medium is able to allocate storage in increments that small). This is because `cpio` is what's called a *streaming* command, meaning that it deals with data as a single continuous stream rather than in chunks of a predefined size.

**RELATED COMMANDS**

`ar, tar`

# cron

## FUNCTION

cron allows you to automate, and schedule with a high degree of control and detail, the execution of programs or shell scripts. You don't accomplish this by running a command at the shell prompt; that's why we haven't included a General Syntax here. Rather, you place entries in a system file, usually located in usr/lib/crontab.

Be aware that on most UNIX systems, only the system administrator, that is, the superuser root, has write privileges on this file, whose entries look like:

```
0 5 * * * /usr//tom/buzz_builder
```

| The parameter . . . | Indicates . . . |
|---|---|
| Column 1 | UNIX will begin to execute a command at this minute. |
| Column 2 | UNIX will begin to execute a command at this hour. |
| Column 3 | UNIX will execute a command on this day of the month. |
| Column 4 | UNIX will execute a command in this month of the year. |
| Column 5 | UNIX will execute a command on this day of the week. |
| Column 6 | UNIX will run this command according to this schedule. |

## SNEAK PREVIEW

```
0 23 * * 1-6 /home/sybase/bin/isql -Uranger -Pfeather -I/home/sybase/interface
-i/home/sybase/cron/11pmtran.in -o/home/sybase/cron/11pmtran.out
~
~
```

## DESCRIPTION

In our example:

```
0 5 * * * /usr//tom/buzz_builder
```

the shell script buzz_builder will run at the 0th minute of the 5th hour of every day of the month, be it a 28- 30-, or 31-day month, every month of the year, every day of the week (Sunday through Saturday).

## RELATED COMMANDS

at, batch

---

# csplit

## FUNCTION

csplit, like split, divides a file into smaller files. However, csplit does so according to some context that you supply to it; that's the origin of the c in the command name.

## GENERAL SYNTAX

```
csplit [-s, -k, -fstring] source-file context
```

| The parameter . . . | Indicates . . . |
|---|---|
| -s | csplit should not include character counts for the files it produces. |
| -k | csplit should not remove files it's already created if it fails to complete its job. |
| -f *string* | csplit should use the *string* supplied with the f option as the name for the files it produces, numbering them sequentially as in, for example, -f*hobo* producing files named hobo00, hobo01, hobo02, and so on. |
| source-file | The file is to be divided. |
| context | The source file will be split at points, which include<br>exp — The first point at which the source file will be split is the first line in the source file that contains the string represented by exp.<br>%exp — The first point at which the source file will be split is the same as that for exp, *but no file will be created for that portion of the source file occurring up to the line containing the string represented by* %exp.<br>1*number* — Our personal favorite, causes the splitting to begin at the line in the source file indicated by *number.* |

## SNEAK PREVIEW

```
# ls -l hobo
hobo not found
#
#
#
# csplit -f hobo specialmsgs 3
2
127
# ls -l hobo*
-rw-rw-rw-  1 root      sys            2 Dec 17 18:28 hobo00
-rw-rw-rw-  1 root      sys          127 Dec 17 18:28 hobo01
```

## DESCRIPTION

`csplit` gives you a high degree of control over the way in which you divvy up a file. But if all you want is a number of files of nearly equal length, `split` will do just as well.

## RELATED COMMANDS

cut, join, paste, split

# cu

## FUNCTION

cu, which stands for *call UNIX*, is one of the family of built-in UNIX data communications commands, which also includes ones such as uucp. The cu command lets you connect to another UNIX machine, either through the phone lines or by a direct cable link.

## GENERAL SYNTAX

cu [options] telephone number *or* line *or* host-name

| The parameter . . . | Indicates . . . |
|---|---|
| options | How cu tries to connect to another UNIX machine; includes the following:<br>l — The line, that is, the name in the form /dev/ttyxxx, of a UNIX device such as the serial port through which the connection will be established.<br>d — Tracing the connection attempt for diagnostic purposes.<br>n — Prompting the user for a telephone number.<br>Note that the n parameter can't be used with line or host-name. |
| telephone number | cu tries to connect to a modem by dialing this phone number. |
| line | line is required with the l option. |
| host-name | host-name represents the name of the remote (even if it's only in the next room) computer to which cu will try to connect. |

## SNEAK PREVIEW

```
#
#
# cu -l/dev/null
Connect failed: Requested device/system name not known
```

## DESCRIPTION

cu, as used in the Sneak Preview, tries to connect to another UNIX machine attached to the serial port designated /dev/ttypa. If you want to use cu like this, make sure there's a cable between the serial port on the machine where you're running cu, and the serial port on the machine to which you're trying to connect. Also, make sure that the cable in question is what's known as a *null-modem cable*, meaning that the cable is built to fool the machines on both ends into thinking there's a modem between them.

## RELATED COMMANDS

uux, uucp, uuto

# cut

## FUNCTION

cut lets you pull out columns or fields from every line in a file, and place those lines to any form of output UNIX accepts.

## GENERAL SYNTAX

```
cut [-c<range >or -f<list >or -d<char >or -s]
```

| The parameter . . . | Indicates . . . |
|---|---|
| -c<range> | cut will pull out and display the range of columns indicated by range, which must be stated as, for example, 20-50, with no interspersed spaces. |
| -f<list> | cut will pull out of every line the fields specified by list, which must be stated as, for instance, 10,13 with no intervening spaces. |
| -d<char> | cut will use the character defined by char as the delimiter for fields that it will yank, as in, for example, d@ causing cut to pull out of a file every field marked off by the @. |
| -s | cut will ignore lines whose fields aren't separated from one another in some way (the s stands for suppress). |

## SNEAK PREVIEW

```
# cat specialmsgs


Nothing here either.
Nothing here either.
Nothing here either.


No new mail so far.
No new mail so far.
No new mail so far.


# cut -c1-6 specialmsgs > cutout
#
# cat cutout


Nothin
Nothin
Nothin


No new
No new
No new
```

## DESCRIPTION

cut, as you see it in the Sneak Preview, makes vertical cuts, or *extractions,* from a file.

## RELATED COMMANDS

csplit, join, paste, split

# date

## FUNCTION

date reports the current date and time as stored in the system clock. If you're the superuser, you can also use date to set that date and time. And in any case, you can control how it is displayed.

## GENERAL SYNTAX

    date +[format]

Or, to set the date:

    date MMDDhhmmYY

| The parameter . . . | Indicates . . . |
|---|---|
| +format | The way in which you wish the date and time to be presented. This parameter must begin with the percent sign (%), and can include scads of indicators. The most common of these are<br><br>a — Causes the day portion of the display to be in an abbreviated format, as in, for example, Sat or Mon.<br>A — Presents the day's name fully, as in Tuesday.<br>b — Presents an abbreviated month name, like Dec.<br>B — Produces a full month name, like January.<br>c — Displays the complete date and time, such as Sat Jan 3 10:22:17 EST 1998.<br>d — Produces the day of the month, such as 03.<br>D — Displays the date in the format MMDDYY.<br>y — Shows the last two digits of the year, such as 98.<br>Y — Shows the year as digits, as in 1998. |
| MMDDhhmmYY | The date and time to which you wish to set the system clock. |

## SNEAK PREVIEW

```
#
# date
Sat Jan  3 11:58:32 EST 1998
#
#
#
# date + %A

# date +%A
Saturday
#
#
# date +%x
01/03/98
#
#
# date +%Y
1998
#
#
# date +%B
January
```

## DESCRIPTION

Note that when you specify a display format to date, the portion of the date or time controlled by the specifier is all you'll see. For example, using +%Y produces only 1998. As the Sneak Preview indicates, the time reported by date reflects the time zone in which your UNIX machine is operating. UNIX is smart enough to detect a date with "disaster-potential," as it were. Take a look at what happened when we tried to set the system clock to a date and time that didn't make sense:

```
date: do you really want to run time backwards?[yes/no]n
Only "yes" will make it take!
```

# dd

## FUNCTION

dd lets you convert files from one format to another, for example turning an ASCII file into an EBCDIC one, or vice versa. Note that the dd command is unusual because it uses the syntax parameter=value rather than the syntax -option value, used by almost all other commands.

## GENERAL SYNTAX

dd [parameter=value]

| The parameter . . . | Indicates . . . |
|---|---|
| parameter | The following are included:<br>if — Input file, as in if=somefile.<br>of — Output file, as in of=anotherfile.<br>ibs — Input block size, as in ibs=512 (handy when you're converting files between systems with differing block sizes).<br>obs — Output block size, as in obs=1024 (ditto on the usefulness).<br>bs — Block size to be used for both input and output.<br>count — Number of input blocks to be processed.<br>conv — Format to which the file or input blocks will be converted, as in conv=ibm. Can also equal ascii, ebcdic, lcase or ucase, meaning that the input will be converted to, respectively, ASCII, EBCDIC, all lowercase, and all uppercase. But *don't* capitalize any of these values for format! |
| value | A specific block size with which dd will work or a format that it will produce in creating its output. |

## SNEAK PREVIEW

```
#
# ls -l someotherfile
someotherfile not found
#
# dd if=somefile ibs=512 of=someotherfile
0+1 records in
0+1 records out
#
# ls -l someotherfile
-rw-rw-rw-   1 root        sys              25 Dec 17 18:49 someotherfile
#
```

## DESCRIPTION

Entering **dd if=somefile ibs=512 of=someotherfile** produced the output you see in the Sneak Preview. That is, it took input in chunks of 512 bytes from the input file called somefile and placed the output it produced in the output file called someotherfile.

## RELATED COMMANDS

od

# df

## FUNCTION

df reports the amount of remaining free storage space on a physical device such as a drive.

## GENERAL SYNTAX

```
df [-t] [file system]
```

| The parameter . . . | Indicates . . . |
|---|---|
| -t | In addition to displaying remaining free space in terms of blocks and *information nodes*, df must report their respective overall totals, as well. An information node is equivalent to room enough for one file while a block equals 512 bytes. |
| -file system | A logical organization of data (directories and subdirectories) mounted on a physical device such as a hard drive. |

## SNEAK PREVIEW

```
# df
/backup         (/dev/vg00/backup  ):   522356 blocks    172791 i-node
/home           (/dev/vg00/lvol4   ):   366604 blocks     77992 i-node
/opt            (/dev/vg00/lvol5   ):   294686 blocks     38878 i-node
/tmp            (/dev/vg00/lvol6   ):    54938 blocks     15214 i-node
/usr            (/dev/vg00/lvol7   ):   137698 blocks     39680 i-node
/var            (/dev/vg00/lvol8   ):   263608 blocks     71270 i-node
/stand          (/dev/vg00/lvol1   ):    52842 blocks      7660 i-node
/               (/dev/vg00/lvol3   ):   230570 blocks     22626 i-node
#
```

## DESCRIPTION

As with its counterpart, du, df concerns itself with storage space available. Where du looks at disk space that's in use and reports on what file systems are using that space, df takes the opposite tack, monitoring and reporting on disk space that is free.

## RELATED COMMANDS

du

# diff

## FUNCTION

diff informs you about the differences between one file and another or between one directory and another. What's more, diff also gives you hints on how to make the files or directories the same.

## GENERAL SYNTAX

    diff [options] file1 file2

    or

    diff [options] directory1 directory2

| The parameter . . . | Indicates . . . |
|---|---|
| file1 or directory1 | You think this file or directory may need to be changed to bring it into agreement with file2 or directory2. |
| file2 or directory2 | This file or directory serves as the basis for the comparison. |
| options | Includes, as do so many UNIX commands, more wrinkles than you can shake a stick at. Some of these even generate a script that may be used by the UNIX editor ed to modify the first file. But many of the options to diff are pretty far out, so we suggest you stick with the ones shown in the Sneak Preview. We use the option -C, because it allows you to specify the number of ways in which the files you're comparing differ. |

## SNEAK PREVIEW

```
#
# cat testdiff
This is a test file.
#
# cat testdif2
This is another test file.
#
# diff testdiff testdif2
1c1
< This is a test file.
---
> This is another test file.
```

## DESCRIPTION

diff, unlike other UNIX commands such as cmp, which also compare material, can only work with text, not with object or binary files. But most frequently, text is what you'll want to compare. As you can see in the Sneak Preview, diff points out the following to you:

- Lines that differ between files
- The content of the differing line in the file to be changed (notice the < and remember its role as an indicator of input)
- The UNIX code you must supply to bring the line into agreement with its peer in the template file (this time, think output, and pay attention to the >)

## RELATED COMMANDS

cmp, comm, dircmp, patch

---

# dircmp

## FUNCTION

dircmp allows you to compare directories in a way similar to that in which cmp compares files.

## GENERAL SYNTAX

    dircmp [-d] [-s] [-wn] dir1 dir2

| The parameter . . . | Indicates . . . |
| --- | --- |
| -d | You want to compare contents of files in two directories when those files have the same names. A list like that produced by diff will also be generated, describing what must be done to make said files identical. |
| -s | Messages regarding identical files will not be displayed. |
| -wn | The width of the display line has changed to *n* characters. |
| dir1 | dir1 files will be compared against dir2. |
| dir2 | dir2 files will be compared against dir1. |

## SNEAK PREVIEW

    # dircmp tep1 tep2|more

    Dec 17 18:58 1997  tep1 only and tep2 only Page 1

    ./test1                                  ./test2

## DESCRIPTION

Typing **dircmp dir1 dir2** queries whether files with the same names in dir1 and dir2 are identical in content. The output lists them as the same, if they are; otherwise, they are listed as different. Files of differing names are also noted. For example, entering the command **dircmp /tep1 /tep2|more** produces the results shown in the Sneak Preview (tep1 and tep2 are directories).

If you use -d with dircmp, the display will indicate where the files need to be changed so that the contents become identical, as well. The < or [ characters indicate where changes need to be made in the first file, while the > or ] characters tell you where you must make changes in the second file.

## RELATED COMMANDS

cmp, comm, diff

# dirname

## FUNCTION

dirname outputs all parts of a path name except the most deeply nested subdirectory.

## GENERAL SYNTAX

```
dirname [string]
```

| The parameter ... | Indicates ... |
|---|---|
| string | A directory path within a file system, such as /usr/bin/xpg4 |

## SNEAK PREVIEW

```
# dirname /usr/bin/xpg4
/usr/bin
#
```

## DESCRIPTION

dirname could be considered first cousin to basename. When you want the innermost level of a path name returned, use basename. When you want all *except* the innermost level returned, you must use dirname, as we do in the Sneak Preview.

## RELATED COMMANDS

basename

# du

## FUNCTION

du lets you monitor hard disk usage.

## GENERAL SYNTAX

```
du [-a] [-r] [-s] names
```

| The parameter ... | Indicates ... |
|---|---|
| -a | Nondirectories presented as arguments are displayed. |
| -r | du will display messages about unreadable directories or files that aren't open. |
| -s | Only the total number of blocks will be output. |
| names | This parameter requests all filenames and directories within a specified path. |

## SNEAK PREVIEW

```
# du -s /etc
3518    /etc
#
# du /etc|more
230     /etc/lvmconf
6       /etc/opt/PEX5
2       /etc/opt/audio
2       /etc/opt/dce/security
2       /etc/opt/dce/zoneinfo
190     /etc/opt/dce
8       /etc/opt/starbase
208     /etc/opt
4       /etc/vue/config/types/tools/System_Info
10      /etc/vue/config/types/tools/System_Admin
8       /etc/vue/config/types/tools/Media
24      /etc/vue/config/types/tools
42      /etc/vue/config/types
6       /etc/vue/config/Xsession.d
50      /etc/vue/config
40      /etc/vue/icons/Color
110     /etc/vue/icons
162     /etc/vue
726     /etc/hpC2400
4       /etc/switch
16      /etc/eisa
10      /etc/skel
134     /etc/rc.config.d
```

## DESCRIPTION

As with so many UNIX commands, du is extremely effective when used without any of its parameters. For instance, if we want to know the allocation or disk usage of the /etc directory path, all we need to type is **du /etc**.

Line after line of block size as it relates to both directory and file is revealed to the intrepid viewer. However, some of you out there may want your du without a lot of frills. In this case, -s is a handy little guy to know. To achieve a minimal yet accurate result, enter **du -s /etc**.

Long and drawn-out, or quick and to the point — you choose.

## RELATED COMMANDS

df, ls

# echo

## FUNCTION

echo does just what its name suggests; it repeats, on your monitor, any string given to it. The other parameters described below simply provide display control.

## GENERAL SYNTAX

```
echo [string] [\a \b \c \f \n \r \t \v]
```

| The parameter . . . | Indicates . . . |
| --- | --- |
| string | The message or characters you want written to the screen |
| \a | An alert character (usually the PC bell) |
| \b | A backspace |
| \c | No new line character in your message |
| \f | A form feed |
| \n | An advance to a new line |
| \r | A carriage return |
| \t | A tab |
| \v | A vertical tab |

## SNEAK PREVIEW

```
#
# echo "I admit it — I'm a Trekker."
I admit it — I'm a Trekker.
#
# echo "\t""\t""\t""I admit it — I'm a Trekker."
                    I admit it — I'm a Trekker.
#
```

## DESCRIPTION

As you can see from the Sneak Preview, echo can produce either simple or polished effects. For instance, if you wanted the string:

```
I admit it - I'm a Trekker.
```

to be displayed, beginning in the 15th column position on your monitor, you could type **echo "\t""\t""\t" I admit it - I'm a Trekker."** and press Enter.

If you want to put this to the test, be careful. This example isn't missing any spaces. Nor are there any superfluous double quotation marks ("). echo is picky in how it expects display-control characters to be submitted to it. If you place any spaces

---

in the string just shown, those spaces will be echoed on your monitor, just where you typed them. In the same way, if you don't place double quotes around one of the tab indicators (\t), you won't get a tab at that point in your output. Instead, you'll simply get the characters \t.

One last word of caution about echo: while the syntax and description we're presenting hold true on most flavors of UNIX, this command may not work in a few others.

**RELATED COMMANDS**

banner, cat

# egrep

## FUNCTION

egrep, one of the UNIX triplet of "get regular expression" commands, lets you grab or locate lines that contain a specific pattern of characters.

## GENERAL SYNTAX

    egrep [options] patterns [files]

| The parameter . . . | Indicates . . . |
|---|---|
| options | That the following are included:<br>v — All *nonmatching* lines will be output.<br>c — Only a count of matching lines will be presented.<br>l — Only the names of files containing matching lines will be shown.<br>n — A line number will be prefixed to every matching line that is located and displayed.<br>f*file* — The pattern for which egrep will try to find matches will be taken from the file designated by *file* (no typo here - f and *file* must be smack up against one another).<br>i — egrep will ignore UNIX's usual distinction between upper- and lower-case letters when looking for matches. |
| patterns | egrep will try to find matches for this string (or strings) in its input. |
| files | You want egrep to look for matches in this file (or files) with the string or strings defined by patterns. |

## SNEAK PREVIEW

```
# cat 4egrep
abc
def
abc
bcd
aaa
# egrep aaa 4egrep
aaa
#
```

## DESCRIPTION

egrep, which stands for *extended get regular expression*, like its siblings fgrep and grep, works with regular expressions. A *regular expression* is a standardized way of representing strings whose content may vary. Such representations make use of UNIX *wild-cards* and *metacharacters*. What makes egrep extended? The fact that it can take its input from, or place its output in, either standard input or a file. grep ordinarily works with the former, and fgrep with the latter.

## RELATED COMMANDS

fgrep, grep

---

# export

## FUNCTION

export maps a particular environment variable to your station or PC.

## GENERAL SYNTAX

export VARIABLE

| The parameter . . . | Indicates . . . |
|---|---|
| VARIABLE | A reserved-name UNIX environmental variable such as TERM, or terminal type, which can be any standard terminal emulation such as VT100, VT220, and so on |

## SNEAK PREVIEW

```
# TERM=vt320
#
# export TERM
#
```

## DESCRIPTION

export enables your local PC or terminal to assume the operating characteristics of the particular terminal emulation assigned to it. When you perform a remote login to UNIX, the operating system may see your machine as an unknown terminal type. And, while this in itself is not problematic, there may be instances where things might not work as they should. For instance, you may want to clear the screen and instead get little or no result. A simple walk through a two-step sequence will avert any potential annoyances. Type **TERM=terminal type**. In this line you load an environmental variable with a specific terminal type. We now need to deliver the information to UNIX by typing **export TERM**.

# false

## FUNCTION

false forces a shell script to return a nonzero value, mimicking a command that has failed.

## GENERAL SYNTAX

```
false
```

| The parameter . . . | Indicates . . . |
|---------------------|-----------------|
| false | You're forcing UNIX to behave as if a real command or test had failed. |

## SNEAK PREVIEW

We've included no figure with this command, since the ways in which it can be used vary greatly.

## DESCRIPTION

However you use false, it will return a nonzero value, which is UNIX's way of signaling, when a command has finished executing, that the command has failed. Using it in a shell script would go something like this:

```
if false
#here, false is just a placeholder which will later be
#replaced with real test of some kind
then
     echo Red Alert
#likewise, this message will be replaced, in the final
#version of the shellscript, with a real error or warning message
     exit 1
#but in either case, the shellscript will return a non-zero value,
#which under UNIX indicates an error
fi
```

## RELATED COMMANDS

sh, test, true

# fgrep

## FUNCTION
fgrep looks for strings that match a regular expression. Usually, it looks in a file.

## GENERAL SYNTAX
    fgrep [options] patterns [files]

| The parameter . . . | Indicates . . . |
| --- | --- |
| options | That the following are included:<br>v — Outputs all *nonmatching* lines<br>x — Displays any matching lines in their entirety<br>c — Presents only a count of matching lines<br>l — Shows only the names of files containing matching lines<br>n — Prefixes a line number to every matching line that is located and displayed<br>f*file* — Takes the pattern for which fgrep will try to find matches from the file designated by *file* |
| patterns | The string or strings for which fgrep will try to find matches in its input |
| files | The file or files in which you want fgrep to look for matches with the string or strings defined by patterns |

## SNEAK PREVIEW

```
#
# cat new.htm
JackieChan
JackieChan
#
# fgrep han new.htm
JackieChan
JackieChan
#
# fgrep -c Chan new.htm
2
# fgrep -v Jackie new.htm
#
# fgrep -n ackie new.htm
1:JackieChan
2:JackieChan
#
```

## DESCRIPTION
fgrep, unlike grep, can't work with metacharacters (special characters such as ? and $, which have special meaning and indicate particular actions to be taken). Nor can fgrep match an expression against an area that extends across more than one line in a file. But, like egrep, fgrep can look for more than one pattern simultaneously.

## RELATED COMMANDS
egrep, grep

---

# find

## FUNCTION

find helps you locate files within a path.

## GENERAL SYNTAX

    find [options] path -name string [-print]

| The parameter ... | Indicates ... |
|---|---|
| options | You want find to apply particular characteristics in doing its thing. The most useful of these are:<br>■ -type *indicator*, where indicator can be any of the following: f for regular file; d for directory; b for block-special file; c for character-special file, and more<br>■ -user *username*, as in find . -user lb, which will ferret out all files in every directory and subdirectory, including and below the current one, which belongs to the user lb |
| path | You want find to search for files in this portion of the file system. |
| -name string | This is not an option, but rather, the string you supply should be contained in the names of files find reports to you. |
| -print | Once again, this is not an option, but rather that you want find to display its results. On some UNIX systems, if you don't include this parameter, find won't say a word. Just to be sure, we recommend you always use this option. |

## SNEAK PREVIEW

```
# find . -name .profile
./etc/skel/.profile
./home/sybase/.profile
./usr/newconfig/etc/skel/.profile
./usr/newconfig/.profile
./.profile
#
# find . -name '*profil?' -print
./etc/d.profile
./etc/skel/.profile
./etc/profile
./home/sybase/.profile
./usr/newconfig/etc/skel/.profile
./usr/newconfig/etc/profile
./usr/newconfig/.profile
./usr/dt/config/sys.dtprofile
./.profile
#
# find /etc -name passwd
/etc/passwd
#
```

## DESCRIPTION

You might say `find` is UNIX's analog to Windows 3.x's File Manager or Windows 95 and NT's Explorer. `find` locates files in the path you specify, which have the string you've supplied in their names.

You may get dozens of filenames scrolling off your screen, depending on the following:

- What that string is
- How extensive your file system is
- What parts of it you tell `find` to search

We recommend that you get in the habit of using `find` in combination with `more`, like this:

```
find . -name '*.htm' | more
```

## RELATED COMMANDS

`ls`

# finger

## FUNCTION

finger tells you about users who have accounts on your system, supplying details such as login name, full name, how long the user has been logged in, how long the user's session has been idle, and more.

## GENERAL SYNTAX

```
finger [options] user(s)
```

| The parameter ... | Indicates ... |
|---|---|
| options | The details of how you want finger to function; includes -b, to suppress displaying a user's home directory; -i, to display login name, login terminal, time the login took place, and how long the session has been idle; -l, to specify that you want to see a long listing, which includes the user's login name, whether he or she wishes to receive messages, what the user's home directory and default shell are, and several characteristics of the current session, -q, to ask that only login name, terminal, and time be presented. |
| user(s) | You want finger to tell you about this user or users. |

## SNEAK PREVIEW

```
#
# finger root
Login name: root             (messages off)
Directory: /                          Shell: /sbin/sh
On since Mar  5 03:13:47 on ttyp2 from 207.103.113.108

No Plan.
# finger -l root
Login name: root             (messages off)
Directory: /                          Shell: /sbin/sh
On since Mar  5 03:13:47 on ttyp2 from 207.103.113.108

No Plan.
# finger -i root
Login     TTY              When             Idle
root      *ttyp2           Thu Mar  5 03:13
# finger -q root
Login     TTY              When
root       ttyp2           Thu Mar  5 03:13
#
```

## DESCRIPTION

The *plan* referred to in the Sneak Preview refers to a file in the inquired-about user's home directory that is the analog, available in many versions of UNIX, to a groupware application's project-planning and control file. The statement (messages off) that you see there means that the user root has used the `mesg` command to preclude his or her receiving messages generated by such commands as `write` and `wall`. Otherwise, `finger`'s output is pretty self-explanatory. The only thing you have to ponder is just how much information about a particular user you'd like to receive.

If you are connected to the Internet, `finger` can also provide information about users on another computer network (if their security allows a response to your query).

## RELATED COMMANDS

`mail, wall, who, write`

# ftp

## FUNCTION

ftp, short for *File Transfer Protocol,* allows you to move files to and from remote systems on which you have an account. This command starts an interactive session in which you can use the commands listed in the table.

## GENERAL SYNTAX

```
ftp host name or host IP address
[ascii] [binary] [bell] [cd remotedir]
get filelist or put filelist
bye
```

| The parameter . . . | Indicates . . . |
|---|---|
| host name | You wish to transfer files to or from this remote server with ftp. |
| host IP address | This Internet protocol or four-part address, such as 207.103.130.119, tells ftp and any other member of the TCP/IP family of utilities the host to which you want to connect. |
| ascii | You want to transfer files as ASCII text. |
| binary | You want to transfer files as binary. |
| bell | You want ftp to ring the PC's bell after each transfer. |
| cd remotedir | You want to change to the indicated directory on the remote machine before transferring files. |
| get | You want ftp to transfer a file from the remote host into the current working directory on the local host. |
| put | You want to transfer a file from the current working directory on the local host to the current directory on the remote host. |
| filelist | You want to transfer this file or files with ftp. |
| bye | You want to end your ftp session. |

## SNEAK PREVIEW

```
# ftp 207.103.0.2
ftp: connect: Connection refused
ftp> bye
#
```

## DESCRIPTION

Like cc, make, and telnet, ftp isn't — properly speaking — part of UNIX. But you'd have to look long and hard to find a UNIX environment that lacks this command.

In order to use ftp, you usually have an account on the remote system with which you want to exchange files, and are in the local directory from or to which you wish to transfer. Many publicly available FTP servers allow you to log in as user "anonymous" with your e-mail address as your password.

As the Sneak Preview attempts to show, if both of these are the case *and* the server to which you're trying to connect is active, then a sequence such as

```
ftp 207.103.113.182
put anewfile
```

would place the file called anewfile in your default directory on the remote machine.

## RELATED COMMANDS

telnet

# getopts

## FUNCTION
getopts examines command lines to determine if the options they contain are allowed with the command in question.

## GENERAL SYNTAX
```
getopts options-list variable
```

| The parameter ... | Indicates ... |
|---|---|
| options-list | The options for which you wish getopts to search |
| variable | The shell variable to which getopts will assign processing results |

## SNEAK PREVIEW
Like false, getopts doesn't have a screen shot because it is mostly used within shell scripts.

## DESCRIPTION
getopts looks for any of the options x, y, or z in the command line it examines, and places any it finds in the standard shell variable opt. If getopts finds no matches for members of its options list, it instead places the value ? in opt, indicating that no valid options were used with the command.

getopts is most frequently used in shell scripts to alert users to invalid options. For example:

```
while getopts xyz: OPT
do
#as long as there are options for getopts to examine
    case $opt in
#look at every value which the variable opt might hold
            x) flagx=TRUE ;;
            y) flagy=TRUE;;
            z) flagz=TRUE;;
#if that value is anything other than x, ,y, or z
            \?) echo $MESSAGE;;
#print the message you stored earlier
    esac
#don't consider any other possible values for OPT
done
#and quit looping through the options the user typed
```

## RELATED COMMANDS
false, sh, test, true

---

*Hip Pocket Guide to UNIX*

# grep

## FUNCTION

grep, which stands for *get regular expression,* looks for matches with a string.

## GENERAL SYNTAX

    grep [options] patterns [files]

| The parameter . . . | Indicates . . . |
| --- | --- |
| options | The following are included:<br>s — Error messages will be suppressed.<br>i — Differences between upper and lower case will be ignored in looking for matches.<br>v — All *nonmatching* lines will be displayed.<br>x — Any matching lines will be presented in their entirety.<br>c — Only a count of matching lines will be produced.<br>l — Only the names of files containing matching lines will be shown.<br>q — grep will keep quiet and produce no display, but it will generate an exit status. As you can imagine, this option is useful only in shell scripts.<br>n — A line number will be prefixed to every matching line that is located and displayed. |
| patterns | grep will try to match the string or strings. |
| files | grep will seek matches in the file or files. |

## SNEAK PREVIEW

```
#
# ls -l profile
-r--r--r--   1 bin        bin           972 Jun 10  1996 .profile
#
# ls -l | grep -c .profile
1
#
# ls -l | grep -n .profile
2:-r--r--r--   1 bin        bin           972 Jun 10  1996 .profile
#
```

## DESCRIPTION

grep, the granddaddy of the UNIX pattern-matching clan, searches through whatever you give it as input, either standard input or a file, for lines matching a pattern. Then, grep reports back to you about what it's found, in any of a variety of ways.

Note that on some systems, such as the Hewlett-Packard UNIX platform on which we took all our Sneak Preview shots, grep may soon be a clan of one.

## RELATED COMMANDS

egrep, fgrep

# head

## FUNCTION
head presents the first few lines of a file or files.

## GENERAL SYNTAX
    head [-c] [-l] [-n count] [file]

| The parameter ... | Indicates ... |
|---|---|
| -c | The amount of output as measured in bytes. Note, if -n count required two bytes, you would see two alphanumeric characters output. |
| -l | The amount of output as measured in lines. Default is in lines. |
| -n (count) | The actual number of bytes or lines displayed. If a number is not specified for count, a default of 10 is assumed. |
| file | head will process the files or files. |

## SNEAK PREVIEW

```
total 3530
-r--r--r--   1 bin      bin          972 Jun 10  1996 .profile
-rw-------   1 root     sys         2140 Nov  5 13:50 .sh_history
drwxr-xr-x   3 root     root        1024 Jun 10  1996 .sw
drwxr-xr-x   2 root     root          24 Jun 10  1996 SD_CDROM
drwxr-xr-x   3 sybase   root        1024 Nov 20 10:23 backup
lr-xr-xr-t   1 root     sys            8 Jun 10  1996 bin -> /usr/bin
-rw-------   1 root     sys      1758676 Jan  8 07:55 core
dr-xr-xr-x  15 bin      bin         3072 Nov  5 11:01 dev
dr-xr-xr-x  23 bin      bin         5120 Dec 16 11:07 etc
drwxr-xr-x   8 root     root        1024 Jan  3 12:46 home
lr-xr-xr-t   1 root     sys            8 Jun 10  1996 lib -> /usr/lib
drwxr-xr-x   2 root     root        8192 Jun 10  1996 lost+found
-rw-rw-rw-   1 root     sys            0 Jan 10 14:20 1st4book
dr-xr-xr-x   1 root     root         512 Nov  5 11:01 net
dr-xr-xr-x  14 bin      bin         1024 Jun 10  1996 opt
dr-xr-xr-x  12 bin      bin         2048 Nov  5 09:35 sbin
dr-xr-xr-x   4 bin      bin         1024 Jun 10  1996 stand
-rw-rw-rw-   1 root     sys           27 Jan  3 12:17 testdif2
-rw-rw-rw-   1 root     sys           21 Jan  3 12:17 testdiff
drwxrwxrwx   4 bin      bin         1024 Jan 10 13:59 tmp
dr-xr-xr-x   2 root     root          24 Nov  5 11:01 tmp_mnt
dr-xr-xr-x  24 bin      bin         1024 Jun 10  1996 usr
# head -1 1st4book
total 3530
#
```

## DESCRIPTION
Say you forget what is in a certain file and you want to find out what it contains. You do have some choices. The command cat file | more reads the entire contents of the file to standard output (aka the screen). Using more file would accomplish the same thing.

But, if you type **head file**, you get back the first ten lines of the specified file.

# id

## FUNCTION

id returns both your user ID number and group ID number.

## GENERAL SYNTAX

id

## SNEAK PREVIEW

```
# id
uid=0(root) gid=3(sys)
#
```

## DESCRIPTION

This is it, ladies and gentlemen! One of the few times you will ever see a UNIX command that isn't legion by way of parameters. Just two letters, id, give you your user ID number (uid) and your group ID number (gid).

# join

## FUNCTION

join goes through two sorted files, finds lines that have something in common, joins those lines, and unless you tell the command otherwise, puts the results on standard output (that is, your screen).

## GENERAL SYNTAX

```
join [options] file1 file2
```

| The parameter . . . | Indicates . . . |
|---|---|
| options | The details of what join will do; includes the following:<br>-a *number*—Tells join to display any lines from the file specified by number, which can be only 1 or 2, for which there are no matches in the other file.<br>-e *string*—Tells join to replace any empty output with whatever you specify in the parameter *string*.<br>-j *x y*—Tells join to splice its output based on the *y*th field of file x. y can be any appropriate integer, but once again, x can be only 1 or 2.<br>-t *character*—Tells join to use the *character* you specify as the field separator. Ordinarily, join would look for tabs, new lines, or spaces to fill this role. |
| file1 file2 | join will look for matches in these files. |

## SNEAK PREVIEW

```
#
# cat testdiff
This is a test file.
#
# cat testdif2
This is another test file.
#
# join testdiff testdif2
This is a test file. is another test file.
```

## DESCRIPTION

As you can see from the Sneak Preview, join can be considered something of a misnomer. This command doesn't join files as a whole. Instead, it knits together lines that have at least one piece in common.

Notice, too, that join may not produce anything. In the last tweak of the command we did for the Preview, we asked join to begin splicing at the third field of the line from the second file. But that field, the word *another*, didn't occur in the first file, so join had nothing to do. Remember, it only puts together lines that match.

## RELATED COMMANDS

comm, cut, csplit, paste, sort, split

# kill

## FUNCTION

kill gives you the ability to end a process.

## GENERAL SYNTAX

    kill [ -signo ] PID

| The parameter . . . | Indicates . . . |
| --- | --- |
| -signo | The process to be terminated has this signal number applied to it. The default signal number is 15, but using -9 for the signal number assures that the process is killed. |
| PID | The operating system assigns this arbitrary number, the Process ID Number, to identify any ongoing system activity. |

## SNEAK PREVIEW

```
# cat 4kill
while who | grep root > /dev/null
do
    echo Still logged in.
    sleep 4
done
# ./4kill&
[1]     11442
# Still logged in.

# Still logged in.
kill -9 1144Still logged in.
2
[1] + Killed                    <job name not known>
#
```

## DESCRIPTION

kill ends processes. A *process* is any activity running on a UNIX system; all processes are tagged with a unique ID number.

But, kill cannot do the dirty work all by itself. You, the user, must get the Process ID Number from a snitch called ps (for process status). By typing ps -e, you can obtain a list of all currently running processes, together with their ID numbers.

Then all you have to do is set up for the kill. Make sure that the process you wish to kill belongs to you, or that you are superuser. If not, the kill will not succeed. If you answered either in the affirmative, though, you may enter **kill** followed by the Process ID Number. If you want to be sure the hit doesn't fail, enter **kill -9 PID**.

## RELATED COMMANDS

nohup, sleep

# login

## FUNCTION

login lets you start a shell session regardless of whether you're already in one.

## GENERAL SYNTAX

    login [user name] [environment variables]

| The parameter . . . | Indicates . . . |
| --- | --- |
| user name | The user for whom, and with whose session characteristics, the login will take place |
| environment variables | Specific conditions you want to apply to the shell session you're about to invoke |

## SNEAK PREVIEW

```
root       ttyp3       Jan  3 15:11
# tail -1 /etc/passwd
lb::2:2::/home:/sbin/sh
# login lb
Please wait...checking for disk quotas
(c)Copyright 1983-1996 Hewlett-Packard Co.,   All Rights Reserved.
(c)Copyright 1979, 1980, 1983, 1985-1993 The Regents of the Univ. of Californ
(c)Copyright 1980, 1984, 1986 Novell, Inc.
(c)Copyright 1986-1992 Sun Microsystems, Inc.
(c)Copyright 1985, 1986, 1988 Massachusetts Institute of Technology
(c)Copyright 1989-1993  The Open Software Foundation, Inc.
(c)Copyright 1986 Digital Equipment Corp.
(c)Copyright 1990 Motorola, Inc.
(c)Copyright 1990, 1991, 1992 Cornell University
(c)Copyright 1989-1991 The University of Maryland
(c)Copyright 1988 Carnegie Mellon University

                    RESTRICTED RIGHTS LEGEND
Use, duplication, or disclosure by the U.S. Government is subject to
restrictions as set forth in sub-paragraph (c)(1)(ii) of the Rights in
Technical Data and Computer Software clause in DFARS 252.227-7013.


                    Hewlett-Packard Company
                    3000 Hanover Street
                    Palo Alto, CA 94304 U.S.A.

Rights for non-DOD U.S. Government Departments and Agencies are as set
forth in FAR 52.227-19(c)(1,2).
$
```

## DESCRIPTION

login lets you start a user session. As the Sneak Preview illustrates, the new session takes on all the characteristics ordinarily associated with the user in whose name you start it. Also, you can't go back to your original shell. Rather, when you close a session established by login, you leave the system altogether. In most cases you're better off using su than login.

## RELATED COMMANDS

rlogin, su, who

---

# logname

## FUNCTION
logname displays the login name of the user.

## GENERAL SYNTAX
logname

## SNEAK PREVIEW

```
#
# logname
root
#
# who am i
root        ttyp3         Jan   3 15:15
#
```

## DESCRIPTION
Typing logname will display your login name as shown in the Sneak Preview.

## RELATED COMMANDS
who

# lp

## FUNCTION
lp queues files to a printer.

## GENERAL SYNTAX
    lp [options] [files]

| The parameter . . . | Indicates . . . |
|---|---|
| options | Specifics on how lp will place your print job in the printer's queue; including the following:<br><br>-d*printer* — Sends your job to the printer you've specified, not to the default printer.<br><br>-m — Sends mail to the user who submitted the print job when that job is ready.<br><br>-n*copies* — Prints the number of copies indicated.<br><br>-p*priority* — Indicates print job priority; *priority* must be an integer from 0 to 7 inclusive. A priority of 0 is the lowest, while one of 7 will get your print job out almost before you're done keying in the request. |
| files | What you want to print. |

## SNEAK PREVIEW

```
#
# lp -d othrprtr lst4book
#
#
```

## DESCRIPTION
As the Sneak Preview shows, there's more to lp than first meets the eye. This command allows you a fair amount of control over the characteristics your hard copy will take on, and the circumstances amid which it will be produced.

## RELATED COMMANDS
cancel, lpstat (plus lpr and lpq on some systems)

# lpstat

## FUNCTION

lpstat, which stands for *line printer status,* gives you a number of administrative details on what's happening with a printer.

## GENERAL SYNTAX

```
lpstat [options]
```

| The parameter . . . | Indicates . . . |
|---|---|
| options | Specifics on what you want lpstat to report upon; includes the following:<br><br>dprinter — Telling lpstat that you want status information on the destination printer you've indicated<br><br>o — Asking for the status of specific output requests, that is, print jobs<br><br>p — Telling lpstat you want to inquire about the status of all printers<br><br>-r — Inquiring about the status of the printer spooler, that is, of the request scheduler<br><br>-s — Telling lpstat you want summary information, which includes output on all the above except specific output requests<br><br>-t — Produces status information on everything lpstat tracks<br><br>-uuser — Asking for the status of print jobs submitted by the specific user you indicate |

## SNEAK PREVIEW

```
#
#lpstat -v
lpstat_sol is solaris 5.5.1
lpstat_sun is sunos 4.1.4
#
```

## DESCRIPTION

As the Sneak Preview shows, lpstat can tell you everything you need to know about a UNIX printer, except its make and model. (Even this mighty OS can't read minds.)

## RELATED COMMANDS

cancel, lp (plus lpr and lpq on some systems)

# ls

## FUNCTION

ls creates listings of files and directories in a number of degrees of detail.

## GENERAL SYNTAX

    ls [options] [file or directory list]

| The parameter . . . | Indicates . . . |
| --- | --- |
| options | Just what you want ls to tell you about files or directories. Includes<br>C — Produces multicolumn output that reads across, rather than down, the columns (the default on most systems).<br>F — Causes ls to place an asterisk after any filename that represents an executable, a slash after each directory, an at sign (@) after any symbolic link, and a pipe symbol after each socket.<br>R — Produces a *recursive* listing, that is, one that lists not only files but also subdirectories and their files, within the current or supplied directory name.<br>-a — Creates a listing that includes such hidden files as .profile, ordinarily not shown by ls.<br>-c — Causes ls to sort its output by the most recent inode modification. (An inode is a means of tracking actual files within a directory, storing their addresses on disk, size, and so on. Think of an inode as somewhat analogous to DOS's File Allocation Table.)<br>-g — Produces a listing of files and directories, which details file access mode, number of links to a file, group affiliation of a file, size of the file in bytes, and the last time a file was modified. Be aware that this option is not available under Linux.<br>-i — Causes every file listed to be preceded by its inode number, the UNIX internal ID for the file.<br>-l — Produces a listing of files and directories, which presents file access mode, number of links to a file, the name of the user who owns the file, the file's group affiliation, the size of the file in bytes, and the last time the file was modified.<br>-m — Lists filenames across the screen, separated by commas, as lines of text.<br>-n — Just like the -l (long listing) option, except that it substitutes owner and group ID numbers for owner and group names.<br>-o — Like -l except that it doesn't give any group-related information.<br>-p — Distinguishes directories from files by placing a forward slash ( / ) after all directory names displayed.<br>-r — Causes ls to reverse its normal sort order, and therefore to present results in descending, rather than ascending, ASCII sequence by filename. |

| The parameter . . . | Indicates . . . |
|---|---|
| | -s — Creates output that talks about file sizes in terms of 512-byte units. |
| | -t — Displays a listing sorted according to modification time, with the most recently modified files presented first. |
| | -u — Causes ls to sort its output in descending order of access time, rather than modification time. Note that this option can only be used in combination with -t and -l. |
| file or directory list | You'd like details about the contents or characteristics of these components of a UNIX file system. |

## SNEAK PREVIEW

```
#
#
#
# ls test*
testdi      testdigg   testdigh
# ls -l test*
-rw-rw-rw-   1 root         sys              0 Jan 26 14:26 testdi
-rw-rw-rw-   1 root         sys            127 Jan 23 10:01 testdigg
-rw-rw-rw-   1 root         sys            105 Jan 23 10:02 testdigh
# ls -o test*
-rw-rw-rw-   1 root              0 Jan 26 14:26 testdi
-rw-rw-rw-   1 root            127 Jan 23 10:01 testdigg
-rw-rw-rw-   1 root            105 Jan 23 10:02 testdigh
# ls -m test*
testdi, testdigg, testdigh
# ls -r test*
testdigh   testdigg   testdi
#
#
#
```

## DESCRIPTION

As the Sneak Preview indicates, ls and its legion of options and option combinations allow you to learn just about everything about what's going on in a UNIX file system.

## RELATED COMMANDS

cd, chgrp, chmod, chown, mount

# mail

## FUNCTION
mail lets you send e-mail to anyone with a user account on your UNIX host or a remote UNIX host.

## GENERAL SYNTAX
    mail [options] user(s)

| The parameter ... | Indicates ... |
|---|---|
| options | Includes, for sending mail: |
| | w — Starts a message on its way to a remote user without waiting for the remote connection to be fully established. On some systems, this option must be expressed as -d, for *direct* delivery. |
| | t — Adds a destination list, of the form *To:* followed by the name of all intended recipients of your message. |
| | Includes, for getting mail |
| | p — Causes mail to sequentially display all messages waiting for you, without giving you the chance to respond to each one individually. |
| | q — Bails out of mail. |
| user(s) | You wish to exchange mail with this user or users. |

## SNEAK PREVIEW

```
# mail -d root
Hello to myself.
#
# mail
From root Wed Jan 14 11:46:03 EST 1998
Hello to myself.

? q
#
# mail -p
From root Wed Jan 14 11:46:03 EST 1998
Hello to myself.
```

## DESCRIPTION
Entering the mail command all by itself at the shell prompt, as the Sneak Preview shows, displays messages one at a time in last-in, first-out order. The ? is mail's way of saying "What shall I do next?" To delete the message you've just viewed from your mailbox, enter **d** at the ? prompt. To see the next message, if any, press Enter.

## RELATED COMMANDS
finger, who

---

# make

## FUNCTION

make is related to cc and is not a part of UNIX proper. make allows you to create and use batch files called *makefiles*, through which you can automate and control C source code compilation.

## GENERAL SYNTAX

```
make
```

## SNEAK PREVIEW

```
# ls -l makefile
-rwx------   1 root        sys              46 Jan 14 13:25 makefile
#
# cat makefile
hithere: hithere.c
        cc -c hithere.c -ohithere
#
# make
'hithere' is up to date.
#
```

## DESCRIPTION

When we discussed the command cc, we wrote the little C program hithere .c, which creates the single line of output, *Hi there, everybody!* If we want to create an object file whose name is the same as our source file, we have two choices. We can either enter **cc -c hithere.c -ohithere** at the UNIX prompt, or we can create a file called makefile in our home directory, which contains that same command. Then, simply typing **make** accomplishes everything the previous example did.

make is ordinarily used to automate the compilation and linking of an executable that draws on several C modules. A more likely makefile might look like this:

```
hithere:    hithere.c module2.c module3.c
        cc -c hithere.c module2.c module3.c -o hithere
```

The first line of this more realistic makefile defines the executable to be produced, as well as the files (either C source or object, that is, .o, files created from such source) upon which this executable depends, giving this line its more formal moniker of *dependency*. The second line, as you can see, explicitly lays out the syntax of the compilation.

make, as the Sneak Preview shows, won't recompile or relink executables whose components haven't changed since the last time the executable was created. Those spaces in front of the cc command in the second line of our simple makefile are actually a single tab. make, at least under HP-UX 10.2 where we tested this command, wants this single character at the beginning of any line in a makefile that conveys compilation and linking instructions.

## RELATED COMMANDS

cc

---

# man

## FUNCTION

man displays UNIX user manual pages for the commands you specify, as well as for special UNIX files such as /etc/passwd, and even for library functions and high-level, administrative commands.

## GENERAL SYNTAX

man command-name

| The parameter . . . | Indicates . . . |
|---|---|
| command-name | You want to review this UNIX command's online documentation. |

## SNEAK PREVIEW

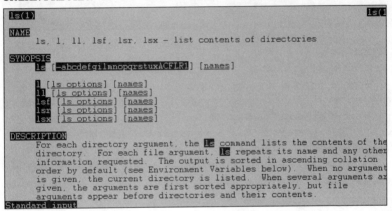

```
ls(1)                                                                    ls(1
NAME
      ls, l, ll, lsf, lsr, lsx - list contents of directories

SYNOPSIS
      ls [-abcdefgilmnopqrstuxACFLR1] [names]

      l  [ls options] [names]
      ll [ls options] [names]
      lsf [ls options] [names]
      lsr [ls options] [names]
      lsx [ls options] [names]

DESCRIPTION
      For each directory argument, the ls command lists the contents of the
      directory.  For each file argument, ls repeats its name and any other
      information requested.  The output is sorted in ascending collation
      order by default (see Environment Variables below).  When no argument
      is given, the current directory is listed.  When several arguments ar
      given, the arguments are first sorted appropriately, but file
      arguments appear before directories and their contents.
Standard input
```

## DESCRIPTION

Be forewarned: man's output isn't the friendliest in the world. But for details and version-specific quirks of every UNIX command you can imagine and more, man is the ultimate source. As you can see from the Sneak Preview, man's output, considered a form of standard output, is automatically paged. To see the rest of man's (usually extensive) displays, you can press Enter to proceed one line at a time, or the spacebar to get another screenful of man's offerings.

# mesg

## FUNCTION

mesg allows you to make your terminal or PC available or unavailable to the write command. If only dealing with other junk mail were as easy!

## GENERAL SYNTAX

```
mesg [n] [y]
```

| The parameter . . . | Indicates . . . |
|---|---|
| n | You don't want any messages. |
| y | You want messages. |

## SNEAK PREVIEW

```
# mesg
is n
# mesg y
# mesg
is y
# write root

        Message from root (ttyp2) [ Mon Mar 02 23:18:45 ]
Hello there!
Hello there!
<EOT>
#
```

## DESCRIPTION

UNIX gives you several ways to communicate with other users logged in to the same host; such commands include talk, wall, and write. If you don't want to receive such messages, you can forego them by using the command line mesg n. With no parameters, typing **mesg** tells you whether your terminal can receive messages.

## RELATED COMMANDS

wall, who, write, talk

# mkdir

## FUNCTION

mkdir creates new directories (within the current working directory, unless you specify otherwise).

## GENERAL SYNTAX

```
mkdir [-m access mode] [-p] new directory name
```

| The parameter . . . | Indicates . . . |
|---|---|
| -m access mode | You want UNIX to set access permission to whatever you specify on the directory it will create. |
| -p | mkdir should create any intervening directories if they don't already exist. |
| new directory name | You want this name assigned to your new directory. It can be a simple, relative, or full path name. |

## SNEAK PREVIEW

```
# pwd
/
# ls -l peace
peace not found
# mkdir peace
# ls -d peace
peace
#
```

## DESCRIPTION

Most frequently, mkdir is used to conjure up new subdirectories within an existing directory. But if used with a full path name, it can make directories anywhere. In either case, though, you must have write permission on the directory within which you want to create a new one, or mkdir will fail.

## RELATED COMMANDS

chmod, ls, rmdir

# more

## FUNCTION
more displays whatever you give it as input one screen at a time.

## GENERAL SYNTAX
    more filename
    or
    a command | more

| The parameter . . . | Indicates . . . |
|---|---|
| filename | You want UNIX to display the file in nice, easy-to-follow screenfuls. |

## SNEAK PREVIEW
```
# more testdiff
This is a test file.
testdiff: END
#
```

## DESCRIPTION
Any time you expect extensive output and want to prevent its scrolling away before you can even begin to focus on it, use more. But be aware, as the Sneak Preview hints, that when you ask more to display something that wouldn't have taken up much of the screen, more still assumes it will, and

- clears the screen in preparation
- forces you to press Enter, the spacebar, or Ctrl+C as appropriate, in order to return to the shell prompt

## RELATED COMMANDS
cat, grep, ls, ps

# mv

## FUNCTION
mv lets you move or rename a file or directory.

## GENERAL SYNTAX
```
mv [-f] old name new name
```

| The parameter ... | Indicates ... |
|---|---|
| -f | You want mv to forego its usual practice of asking you for further instructions when you supply it a file or directory for which you don't have write permission. |
| old name | For a file, the name of the file that you wish to change; for a directory, the directory whose name you want to change. |
| new name | For a file, can be a simple, relative, or full path name. |

## SNEAK PREVIEW

```
# ls
.profile      bin         hithere.c    net         stand       usr
.sh_history   core        home         newdir      testdif2    var
.sw           dev         lib          old_dir     testdiff
5D_CDROM      etc         lost+found   opt         tmp
backup        hithere     makefile     sbin        tmp_mnt
# mv testdiff testdigg
# ls
.profile      bin         hithere.c    net         stand       usr
.sh_history   core        home         newdir      testdif2    var
.sw           dev         lib          old_dir     testdigg
5D_CDROM      etc         lost+found   opt         tmp
backup        hithere     makefile     sbin        tmp_mnt
#
# mv newdir newerdir
# ls
.profile      bin         hithere.c    net         stand       usr
.sh_history   core        home         newerdir    testdif2    var
.sw           dev         lib          old_dir     testdigg
5D_CDROM      etc         lost+found   opt         tmp
backup        hithere     makefile     sbin        tmp_mnt
#
```

## DESCRIPTION
If you enter **mv testdiff testdigg**, and the file testdiff is in your current working directory, you have write permission for that directory, and you have write permission for that file, then testdiff will cease to exist as a filename and will be replaced by testdigg. You can also use mv to move files or directories to another location within the same file system by entering a new directory path as the new name parameter.

## RELATED COMMANDS
cp, rm

# newgrp

## FUNCTION

newgrp lets you temporarily change your user group affiliation.

## GENERAL SYNTAX

```
newgrp [-] [group name]
```

| The parameter . . . | Indicates . . . |
| --- | --- |
| - | newgrp should reset your group affiliation to the value that would result if you logged in and created a new default-environment session. |
| group name | You want to join this user group. If you don't supply this argument, newgrp resets your membership to the default specified for you in the file /etc/passwd, for the duration of your current session. |

## SNEAK PREVIEW

```
# newgrp bin
#
# newgrp beeblebrox
Unknown group
#
# newgrp
#
```

## DESCRIPTION

As the Sneak Preview shows, newgrp doesn't report its outcome in any way, unless you supply it the name of a nonexistent group.

If you try to use newgrp to temporarily associate your session with a group, for which you're not listed as a member, in the file /etc/group, the attempt will fail.

When it runs successfully, newgrp creates a new shell with the appropriate environment, as defined for the group to which you've transferred in the file /etc/passwd.

## RELATED COMMANDS

chgrp, chmod, chown, ls

# nice

## FUNCTION
nice lets you run a command that you give it as one of its arguments at the nonstandard priority you supply as the other.

## GENERAL SYNTAX
```
nice [- priority change] command
```

| The parameter . . . | Indicates . . . |
|---|---|
| - priority change | The direction in which, and amount by which, you want nice to change the default priority of execution. |
| command | The command you want to run at the altered priority |

## SNEAK PREVIEW

```
# ps -l
  F S            UID     PID    PPID  C PRI NI      ADDR     SZ    WCHAN TTY         TIM
D
 21 T              0    9618    9164  0 157 24    f24e80     50        - ttyp2       0:0
  1 R              0    9164    9163  0 178 20    af5800     82        - ttyp2       0:0
  1 R              0    9648    9164  5 179 20    c12d00     21        - ttyp2       0:0
  1 S              0    9163     585  0 154 20    b27900     19   38bc90 ttyp2       0:0
netd
 21 T              0    9631    9164  0 157 24    f24280     50        - ttyp2       0:0
 21 T              0    9622    9164  0 157 24    c27a80     50        - ttyp2       0:0
# nice -15 ksh
# ps -l
  F S            UID     PID    PPID  C PRI NI      ADDR     SZ    WCHAN TTY         TIM
D
 21 T              0    9618    9164  0 157 24    f24e80     50        - ttyp2       0:0
  1 S              0    9164    9163  0 158 20    af5800     82   6f11c0 ttyp2       0:0
  1 R              0    9649    9164 18 212 35    c7d880     38        - ttyp2       0:0
  1 S              0    9163     585  0 154 20    b27900     19   38bc90 ttyp2       0:0
netd
 21 T              0    9631    9164  0 157 24    f24280     50        - ttyp2       0:0
 21 T              0    9622    9164  0 157 24    c27a80     50        - ttyp2       0:0
  1 R              0    9650    9649  5 209 35    d25000     21        - ttyp2       0:0
#
```

```
-l
          UID     PID    PPID  C PRI NI      ADDR     SZ    WCHAN TTY           TIME COM
            0    9618    9164  0 157 24    f24e80     50        - ttyp2         0:00 ls
            0    9164    9163  0 178 20    af5800     82        - ttyp2         0:02 sh
            0    9648    9164  5 179 20    c12d00     21        - ttyp2         0:00 ps
            0    9163     585  0 154 20    b27900     19   38bc90 ttyp2         0:00 tel

            0    9631    9164  0 157 24    f24280     50        - ttyp2         0:00 ls
            0    9622    9164  0 157 24    c27a80     50        - ttyp2         0:00 ls
e -15 ksh
-l
          UID     PID    PPID  C PRI NI      ADDR     SZ    WCHAN TTY           TIME COM
            0    9618    9164  0 157 24    f24e80     50        - ttyp2         0:00 ls
            0    9164    9163  0 158 20    af5800     82   6f11c0 ttyp2         0:02 sh
            0    9649    9164 18 212 35    c7d880     38        - ttyp2         0:00 ksh
            0    9163     585  0 154 20    b27900     19   38bc90 ttyp2         0:00 tel

            0    9631    9164  0 157 24    f24280     50        - ttyp2         0:00 ls
            0    9622    9164  0 157 24    c27a80     50        - ttyp2         0:00 ls
            0    9650    9649  5 209 35    d25000     21        - ttyp2         0:00 ps
```

## DESCRIPTION

Remember that under UNIX the lower the numeric value that represents a process's execution priority, the higher that process's priority. For instance, a process with a nice value of 5 will run sooner and complete more quickly than one with a value of 6. This being the case, be careful with `nice`. Supplying it unsigned integers as the priority-change parameter will cause it to increase the nice value by the amount you've specified, thereby making the associated command sit even lower on the execution totem pole. Trouble is, you must have superuser privileges to decrement a `nice` value and thereby raise a process's priority of execution. `nice` can't be used by just anybody.

## RELATED COMMANDS

ps

# nohup

## FUNCTION

nohup, which stands for *no hang up*, allows you to guarantee that the command or commands you give it as arguments won't be interrupted as they execute.

## GENERAL SYNTAX

```
nohup command [arguments]
```

| The parameter . . . | Indicates . . . |
|---|---|
| command | The UNIX command you wish to ensure will run to completion, without interruption. |
| arguments | Any arguments required by, or applicable to, the command you want nohup to monitor; these arguments don't apply to nohup itself. |

## SNEAK PREVIEW

```
#
# nohup ./simplscrpt
Sending output to nohup.out
#
# cat nohup.out

This is an example of using
nohup with a shellscript.

This is an example of using
nohup with a shellscript.

This is an example of using
nohup with a shellscript.
#
```

## DESCRIPTION

nohup is particularly useful when applied to UNIX's built-in networking commands, such as cu. nohup can be used with any command, though. nohup is often used to ensure that pipes aren't broken. You'll notice too, from the Sneak Preview, that unless you specifically redirect output, nohup sends its and its partner's results to a file called nohup.out, which is appended to, rather than recreated, every time you run nohup.

If you want to apply nohup to more than one command, you have to type something like **nohup (ps : ls)**

## RELATED COMMANDS

ps

# od

## FUNCTION

od, short for *octal dump,* shows you the contents of a file in any one of a number of forms.

## GENERAL SYNTAX

```
od [-v] [-A base address] [-j skip] [-N counter] [-t type] file
```

| The parameter . . . | Indicates . . . |
|---|---|
| -v | od will use all input data. |
| -A base address | The offset base, that is, the point within the file from which od will begin to gather and display output; possible values are<br>d — The offset address is given in decimal format.<br>o — The offset address is given in octal format.<br>x — The offset address is given in hexadecimal format.<br>n — No offset address is given. |
| -j skip | od should ignore (or jump over) the number of bytes at the beginning of its input, represented by counter, before it begins its display. |
| -N counter | od will present no more than the number of bytes represented by counter. |
| -t type | od will work with only the type of input data represented by type; can include<br>a — A named, or specified, character.<br>c — Any character data.<br>d — Any decimal data.<br>f — Any floating point data.<br>o — Any octal data.<br>u — Any unsigned decimal data.<br>x — Any hexadecimal data. |
| file | You want od to work with this file. |

## SNEAK PREVIEW

```
#
# od -tc ./simplscrpt
0000000    e   c   h   o  \n   e   c   h   o       T   h   i
0000020    s       a   n       e   x   a   m   p   l   e
0000040    u   s   i   n   g  \n   e   c   h   o       n   o
0000060        w   i   t   h       a       s   h   e   l   l
0000100    i   p   t   .  \n   e   c   h   o  \n  \n
0000113
#
#
# od -v ./simplscrpt
0000000   0062543 0064157 0005145 0061550 0067440 0052150 006456
0000020   0071440 0060556 0020145 0074141 0066560 0066145 002015
0000040   0072563 0064556 0063412 0062543 0064157 0020156 006755
0000060   0020167 0064564 0064040 0060440 0071550 0062554 006616
0000100   0064560 0072056 0005145 0061550 0067412 0005000
0000113
#
```

## DESCRIPTION

od is handy in helping you to quickly and easily convert from one form of character encoding to another. For example, if you want to see the octal representations for every hexadecimal character in a file, and you want to see them all on one line, you could type **od -tcx1o somefile**.

Or, to see all input data converted to and displayed as octal notation, just use the -v option, and type **od -v somefile**.

As you can see from the Sneak Preview, od attaches line numbers to its output. Those, like its default display format, are in octal notation. Under some versions of UNIX, there's a command called xd, or hexadecimal dump, which operates exactly like od except that it uses hexadecimal notation as its default.

# pack

## FUNCTION

`pack` compresses or packs files in order to reduce their size.

## GENERAL SYNTAX

```
pack file
```

| The parameter . . . | Indicates . . . |
|---------------------|-----------------|
| `file`              | The name of the file you want to compress |

## SNEAK PREVIEW

```
# ls -l core simplscrpt
-rw-------   1 root        sys         1758676 Jan  8 07:55 core
-rwx------   1 root        sys              75 Jan 22 15:36 simpl
#
# pack simplscrpt
pack: simplscrpt: no saving - file unchanged
#
# pack core
pack: core: 52.2% Compression
#
# ls -l core*
-rw-------   1 root        sys          840187 Jan  8 07:55 core.
#
```

## DESCRIPTION

In a nutshell, `pack` is the UNIX analog to `zip` in the DOS and Windows worlds. `pack`'s a little brighter, though; as you can see from the Sneak Preview, `pack` won't do its thing if compressing won't buy you back any appreciable disk real estate. The Sneak Preview also shows you how `pack` names it output — as the original filename and extension plus the additional extension `.z`.

Some UNIX systems now use the `compress` or `gzip` command instead of `pack`. These newer commands use more efficient compression algorithms, but are not available on every system. They will add the file extension `7` or `.gz` (respectively) to a compressed file.

## RELATED COMMANDS

`pcat`, `unpack` (plus `compress`, `uncompress`, `gzip`, `gunzip`, and `zcat` on some UNIX systems)

# passwd

## FUNCTION
`passwd` creates or changes a login password for the user you specify.

## GENERAL SYNTAX
    passwd [user]

| The parameter . . . | Indicates . . . |
|---|---|
| user | The user name for which you wish to create or modify a login password |

## SNEAK PREVIEW

```
#
# cat /etc/passwd
root:pFBKeTy4q990M:0:3::/:/sbin/sh
daemon:*:1:5::/:/sbin/sh
bin:*:2:2::/usr/bin:/sbin/sh
sys:*:3:3::/:
adm:*:4:4::/var/adm:/sbin/sh
uucp:*:5:3::/var/spool/uucppublic:/usr/lbin/uucp/uucico
lp:*:9:7::/var/spool/lp:/sbin/sh
nuucp:*:11:11::/var/spool/uucppublic:/usr/lbin/uucp/uucico
hpdb:*:27:1:ALLBASE:/:/sbin/sh
nobody:*:-2:-24::/:
sybase:N1SRUrGpU3816:101:20:,,,:/home/sybase:/usr/bin/ksh
petedd:QW4J4mlfveUfo:2:2::/home:/sbin/sh
lb::2:2::/home:/sbin/sh
#
```

```
#
# passwd lb
New password:
Re-enter new password:
#
```

## DESCRIPTION
`passwd` lets you create a password, as done in the Sneak Preview. The command also lets you change a password. UNIX doesn't echo what you type in either case. But it asks you to re-enter the password as a means of being sure. Once a password is installed in the system file `/etc/passwd`, it's encrypted so no one can hack it.

To establish or change a password, you must either be the superuser `root`, or the user whose password will be affected. And, the password you supply should meet these criteria:

- The password should have at least six characters.
- The characters that make up the password should be members of the US ASCII character set.

---

*Hip Pocket Guide to UNIX*

- The password should contain at least two letters and one numeric or special character.

- The password should differ from the user's login name.

- A new password should differ from an old one by at least three characters.

**RELATED COMMANDS**

`login`, `who`

---

# paste

## FUNCTION

paste merges corresponding lines from two or more files, or adjoining lines from a single file.

## GENERAL SYNTAX

```
paste [-d character] [-s] [file 1] [file 2]
```

| The parameter ... | Indicates ... |
|---|---|
| -d character | paste should forego its usual replacement of all newline characters, except the last one in its last block of input with tab characters. Instead paste should use the character you specify in the character parameter as a substitute for tab. You'll often use the newline character, \n, for this role. |
| -s | You want paste to put together subsequent lines within a single file, rather than corresponding lines between two files. |
| file 1, file 2 | You want to join lines from this file (or files). |

## SNEAK PREVIEW

```
# cat 4paste
This file will help to demonstrate
# cat 4paste2
demonstrate the command paste.
# paste 4paste 4paste2
This file will help to demonstrate        demonstrate the command pa
#
```

## DESCRIPTION

paste can be thought of as a horizontal analog to cat. While cat can join files vertically, placing them one after the other, paste joins, for example, line 2 of file 1 with line 2 of file 2. Note, too, from the Sneak Preview, that in order to tell paste to substitute a special character such as the newline for its default delimiter the tab, you must *escape* that character — that is, tell UNIX to take the character literally — rather than interpret and execute it as the OS ordinarily would.

## RELATED COMMANDS

cat, split

# pcat

## FUNCTION

To quote man, *pcat does for packed files what cat does for ordinary files.* pcat
temporarily unpacks a file or files and displays them on standard output.

## GENERAL SYNTAX

```
pcat [filename.z or filename]
```

| The parameter . . . | Indicates . . . |
|---|---|
| filename.z or filename | The name of the packed file you want to see |

## SNEAK PREVIEW

```
# ls -l *.z
-rw-------    1 root         sys          840187 Jan  8 07:55 core.z
#
# pcat core.z|more
```

```
^D ault case in putline/ESC CHAR!!  (press RETURN)
M-^ZM-t^P^BpM-p@^P^P^PKM-1M-VM-0^Dzdaemon.42M-O@^CM-^P^A^?
M-~kM-^D^A^DM-^]M-H^DM-^P^K^O^AM-@      M-)M-SPROC^B{^AT@^TM-^^\M
M-x@^UM-^T@^A3M-M-^D^@^AM-PS^M-^D^G{M-8@^AKM-t@^W^OM-|cnno
M-^?M-^?M-^?M-^?NOPROC@M-|M-0cn`M-^?M-x{^CM-KM-0ESS ^XM-@
M-DM-gM-^?M-^?M-^?M-~KyM-OPROG^D^O^O^B^?M-NyM-O*M-oM-^?M-^?M-^?M
M-^?M-^?M-^?M-^?^?^A^A^F^TM-OgM-1M-zM-OgM-1M-z^GM-i^DM-^^@nM- @nM-
^P^P^?M-^?M-^?^?M-^?M-^?A@M-^@^?M-^?M-^?M-^?^?M-^?M-^?M-
^?M-^?M-^?M-^?^?^?M-^?M-^?M-^?M->M-5M-^XM-9^ZM-g7L?M-w^^M-^KM-X}M-
M-^AnGM-^FM-^HzM-^Y@,M-pM-?-BM-WyM-i^_?M-w^_uM-hM-1 tM-@M-^IM-p^
#
```

## DESCRIPTION

pcat, because it displays compressed files, by definition displays *big* files. You're
probably best off to use pcat with a pipe to more. And what are all those odd
characters you see there? We are displaying a core dump, that is, UNIX's
automatically saving, in the file called core, the contents of memory at a point at
which an important command failed. So, in illustrating both pack and pcat, you're
seeing those contents, rather than easily understood text.

If your system uses the gzip command in place of pack, use zcat instead of pcat.

## RELATED COMMANDS

cat, pack, unpack

---

# pg

## FUNCTION

pg, similar to more, lets you look at material on your screen, one screenful at a time.

## GENERAL SYNTAX

```
pg [-number] [-p string] [-c] [-e] [-f] [-n] [-s] [+ or -line] file(s)
```

| The parameter . . . | Indicates . . . |
|---|---|
| -number | You want each screen displayed in this number of lines. |
| -p string | pg should use the indicated string as its prompt to you. |
| -c | pg should home the cursor, that is, place it at the upper left of the display, and clear the screen between showing you pages of output. |
| -e | pg should not pause, as it ordinarily would, between files it shows you. |
| -f | pg should not split lines it displays, as it ordinarily would. |
| -n | pg should save you the trouble of terminating standard output, by appending a newline character to its display. In other words, it presses the Enter key for you. |
| -s | pg should show you any messages or prompts in standout display, that is, in reverse video. |
| + or -line | pg should start its display at the indicated line number. |
| file(s) | You want to see this file or files. |

## SNEAK PREVIEW

```
# pg +30 4pg
...skipping forward
The Apache Project is a collaborative software development effort aimed
at creating a robust, commercial-grade, featureful, and freely-available
source code implementation of an HTTP (Web) server.  The project is
jointly managed by a group of volunteers located around the world, using
the Internet and the Web to communicate, plan, and develop the server and
its related documentation.  These volunteers are known as the Apache Group.
In addition, hundreds of users have contributed ideas, code, and
documentation to the project.  This file is intended to briefly describe
the history of the Apache Group, recognize the many contributors, and
explain how you can join the fun too.

In February of 1995, the most popular server software on the Web was the
public domain HTTP daemon developed by Rob McCool at the National Center
for Supercomputing Applications, University of Illinois, Urbana-Champaign.
However, development of that httpd had stalled after Rob left NCSA in
mid-1994, and many webmasters had developed their own extensions and bug
fixes that were in need of a common distribution.  A small group of these
webmasters, contacted via private e-mail, gathered together for the purpose
of coordinating their changes (in the form of "patches").  Brian Behlendorf
and Cliff Skolnick put together a mailing list, shared information space,
and logins for the core developers on a machine in the California Bay Area,
with bandwidth and diskspace donated by HotWired and Organic Online.
By the end of February, eight core contributors formed the foundation
#
```

## DESCRIPTION

pg, while it closely resembles more, can go that paginator one better. pg lets you back up through what you've already seen, by using a minus sign in front of its line number indicator. It also clears the screen before each screenful of text is displayed.

## RELATED COMMANDS

cat, more

# pr

## FUNCTION

pr lets you display files on standard output. By default, pr produces output that is divided into pages with each page carrying a header consisting of the page number, the date and time of the display, and the name of the file being displayed.

## GENERAL SYNTAX

```
pr [+x] [-x] [-c x] [-a] [-d] [-m] file(s)
```

| The parameter . . . | Indicates . . . |
|---|---|
| +x | pr should start its display with the page numbered x. |
| -x | pr should produce output presented in x columns. |
| -c x | This command is the same as x. |
| -a | pr should present multicolumn output across the screen; used only with -x or -c x. |
| -d | pr should double-space its output. |
| -m | pr should merge the files you give it as arguments, and present those files one per column; this option overrides -x and -c x. |
| file(s) | You want to see this file or files. |

## SNEAK PREVIEW

```
# cat 4pr
This is a test file.
This is not a test file.
This is another line.
# pr -a -c7 4pr


Mar 04 23:11 1998   4pr Page 1


This is a This is n This is a
```

## DESCRIPTION

pr, like more and pg, is a paginator; it *doesn't* produce hard copy. But it does clear the screen before beginning its display. And if you ask it to show something that's just not there, pr does nothing.

## RELATED COMMANDS

cat, more, pg

# ps

## FUNCTION

ps stands for *process status*. ps gives information about the status of processes, that is, individual tasks, that UNIX is currently handling. ps identifies those processes by their PID or process ID number, a serial number UNIX assigns to every job it does.

## GENERAL SYNTAX

```
ps [-aefl]
```

| The parameter . . . | Indicates . . . |
|---|---|
| -a | That you see information about *all* processes, whether started by the system or a user. However, if you use a, ps won't inform you about processes that aren't directly associated with some terminal. |
| e | That information about all processes is displayed. |
| f | That a *full* listing is presented, displayed with the headers UID PID PPID C STIME TTY TIME COMMAND, which stand for, respectively: <br> UID — The user ID of whoever started the job running. <br> PID — The process ID of the job being tracked. <br> PPID — The process ID of the parent task of the job being tracked. <br> C — The CPU resource percentage required by the job. <br> STIME — The time at which process execution began. <br> TTY — The terminal from which the process was submitted. <br> TIME — The cumulative time the process had been running at the time ps looked at it. <br> COMMAND — The command name (or shell script) represented by PID. |
| l | That a *long* listing is presented, displayed with the headers F S UID PID PPID C PRI NI ADDR SZ WCHAN TTY TIME CMD, which stand for, respectively: <br> F — Special indicators that might be associated with the process; presented as an octal (base 8) number. <br> S — A single-letter abbreviation of a verbal indication of the process status; can be S for sleeping, W for waiting, T for terminated, R for running, and even a few more. <br> UID, PID, PPID, C, TTY, TIME — The same as for a full listing. <br> PRI — The priority at which the job will run. The lower the number, the more immediate UNIX considers the process. <br> NI — The nice value (part of what's needed to determine priority). |

*Continued*

---

*Continued*

| The parameter . . . | Indicates . . . |
|---|---|
| | ADDR — The address in memory where the job lives. |
| | SZ — The amount of memory, given as a number of blocks, that the process is using. |
| | WCHAN — The event, if any, for which the process must wait before it can complete. |
| | CMD — The name of the command (or shell script) represented by PID. |

## SNEAK PREVIEW

```
# ps
   PID TTY       TIME COMMAND
 16618 ttyp3     0:00 sh
 16660 ttyp3     0:00 ps
 16617 ttyp3     0:00 telnetd
#
```

## DESCRIPTION

ps has many options and therefore combinations of actions available. The exact options offered may differ from one flavor of UNIX to another. We'll just discuss here how to determine the process status of jobs running at the terminal to which you've logged on. Typing **ps** and pressing Enter gives you the status of any processes active at, or associated with, the terminal to which you've logged in. This status information is in the form seen in the Sneak Preview.

## RELATED COMMANDS

kill, ls

# pwd

## FUNCTION

pwd gives the name of the working directory.

## GENERAL SYNTAX

pwd

## SNEAK PREVIEW

```
# pwd
/home/httpd/htdocs
#
```

## DESCRIPTION

If you've been enjoying your new-found expertise in UNIX and listing and changing directories, without keeping track of the steps you've taken, it's possible you might end up forgetting your current directory. UNIX has help for you on that score. It's in the form of the command pwd, which means *print working directory*. Issuing this command to UNIX causes it to display to you the full name of the directory in which you're currently working, as you can see from the Sneak Preview.

Note that pwd may behave a bit differently under some of the less-frequently used UNIX shells such as ksh, the Korn shell.

## RELATED COMMANDS

cd, ls

# rlogin

## FUNCTION
`rlogin` lets you log in to a remote UNIX host.

## GENERAL SYNTAX
```
rlogin host [-7] [-8] [-1 user]
```

| The parameter . . . | Indicates . . . |
|---|---|
| host | You wish to connect to, and establish a user session on, this remote UNIX machine. |
| -7 | You want `rlogin` to work in bytes of seven characters as it transmits what you type to the remote host, with any eighth character per byte being set to 0. |
| -8 | You want `rlogin` to work in bytes of eight characters. |
| -1 user | You want `rlogin` to start a remote session under the user name you specify in the parameter `user`. Without this option, `rlogin` uses the name under which you logged on to the local machine. |

## SNEAK PREVIEW
```
# rlogin doli
Password:
Please wait...checking for disk quotas
```

## DESCRIPTION
`rlogin` can even be used to create another shell on a local UNIX host; that's how we created the Sneak Preview.

## RELATED COMMANDS
`login`, `who`

# rm

## FUNCTION

rm is used to delete files or directories.

## GENERAL SYNTAX

```
rm [-I] [-f] [-r] file
```

| The parameter ... | Indicates ... |
|---|---|
| -I | An interactive session where confirmation is required before removing the stated file or directory. |
| -f | That files are removed without asking questions even though write permissions are not available. |
| -r | That a directory is to be removed after first removing its contents. Any subdirectories are emptied first then deleted. |
| file | The name of the file or files to be removed. |

## SNEAK PREVIEW

```
drwxr-xr-x    3 sybase     root          1024 Nov 20 10:23 backup
lr-xr-xr-t    1 root       sys              8 Jun 10  1996 bin -> /usr/bin
-rw-------    1 root       sys        1758676 Jan  8 07:55 core
dr-xr-xr-x   15 bin        bin           3072 Nov  5 11:01 dev
dr-xr-xr-x   23 bin        bin           5120 Dec 16 11:07 etc
drwxr-xr-x    8 root       root          1024 Jan  3 12:46 home
lr-xr-xr-t    1 root       sys              8 Jun 10  1996 lib -> /usr/lib
drwxr-xr-x    2 root       root          8192 Jun 10  1996 lost+found
-rwx------    1 root       bin           3026 Jan 10 14:21 lst4book
dr-xr-xr-x    1 root       root           512 Nov  5 11:01 net
dr-xr-xr-x   14 bin        bin           1024 Jun 10  1996 opt
dr-xr nr-x   12 bin        bin           2048 Nov  5 09:35 sbin
dr-xr-xr-x    4 bin        bin           1024 Jun 10  1996 stand
-rw-rw-rw-    1 root       sys             27 Jan  3 12:17 testdif?
-rw-rw-rw-    1 root       sys             21 Jan  3 12:17 testdiff
drwxrwxrwx    4 bin        bin           1024 Jan 10 16:06 tmp
dr-xr-xr-x    2 root       root            24 Nov  5 11:01 tmp_mnt
dr-xr-xr-x   24 bin        bin           1024 Jun 10  1996 usr
# rm -i lst4book testdiff
lst4book: ? (y/n) y
testdiff: ? (y/n) n
# ls lst4book testdiff
lst4book not found
testdiff
#
```

## DESCRIPTION

rm is a highly useful command with a coterie of equally useful parameters. A word to the wise, however: Make sure you thoroughly understand what those parameters and different forms of the command can do in practice.

We rarely ever say never. But *never* type **rm \***. We really mean this warning! If you don't want all the files in the directory in which you are sitting deleted *forever*, just don't! Instead, use the following command:

```
rm -i <file>
```

In this case, you have a chance to confirm whether you actually want to delete a file for *all eternity*.

Further, while

```
rm -r <directory>
```

might seem like a good bet, think again about what it does. It's like saying, "Okay, I'm going to get rid of all the files in the directory and then smoke the directory, too! And, if there are any subdirectories, I'm going to do the same number on them first!" Use with extreme caution.

We would instead suggest removing the files first using

```
rm -I <file(s)>
```

Then follow this with the `rmdir` command to remove the directory itself. This may be a slower operation, but you have much more opportunity to recover from a mistake in judgment.

## RELATED COMMANDS

```
rmdir
```

# rmdir

## FUNCTION
rmdir removes directories.

## GENERAL SYNTAX
```
rmdir [-f] [-i] [-p] directory or directories
```

| The parameter ... | indicates ... |
| --- | --- |
| -f | rmdir should remove every directory you've specified without checking to confirm that you want those directories deleted. |
| -i | rmdir should operate interactively, prompting you to confirm each deletion you've requested. |
| -p | If the directories you've told it to blow away are all children of the same parent, and if after removing those children the parent directory is empty, rmdir should get rid of the parent, too. |
| directory or directories | You want rmdir to delete this directory or directories. |

## SNEAK PREVIEW
```
#
# ls -d peace
peace
# rmdir peace
# ls -d peace
peace not found
#
```

## DESCRIPTION
To use rmdir, you must have write permission for the directories you want to delete, as well as for any parent directories involved. You can only remove empty directories on most UNIX systems. If the directory appears to be empty but rmdir fails, use the ls command with the -a parameter to check for hidden files.

## RELATED COMMANDS
ls, rm

# sh

## FUNCTION

sh starts a new user shell as a child process of your original one.

## GENERAL SYNTAX

```
sh [command]
```

| The parameter . . . | Indicates . . . |
|---------------------|-----------------|
| command | The command you want your new shell to run |

## SNEAK PREVIEW

```
# cat newscrpt
echo
echo This script will help to demonstrate sh.
echo

# sh; ./newscrpt
#

This script will help to demonstrate sh.

#
```

## DESCRIPTION

Anything you can do in a UNIX shell can be done in a shell established with sh. You can use this command to

- create a different operating environment with its own set of environment variables
- create child processes that have no direct relationship with your original operating environment
- test shell scripts under varying circumstances
- create and work with files that have different access modes than those in your initial shell

If you look closely at the Sneak Preview, you'll see that, when we used sh to start a new shell, the shell script we tried to run was unavailable. Only after we left the child shell and returned to the parent did newscrpt run.

# sleep

## FUNCTION

sleep suspends task execution for a specified period of time.

## GENERAL SYNTAX

```
sleep time
```

| The parameter . . . | Indicates . . . |
|---|---|
| time | The period (in seconds) UNIX will wait before resuming work on the command |

## SNEAK PREVIEW

```
# date
Mon Mar  2 23:44:40 EST 1998
# sleep 17; ls; date
.profile          file1             newscrpt
.sh_history       file3             nohup.out
.sw               find_trek_files   old_dir
4egrep            find_trek_files_2 oldstuf
4sort             from_grep         opt
4sort2            hithere.c         phn_book
4spell            home              phn_1st
SD_CDROM          hoover            progenv_1
backup            lib               sbin
bin               lost+found        stand
buzz-builder      lp                testdi
core              menu_vac          testdigg
dev               net               testdigh
etc               newfile           tmp
Mon Mar  2 23:45:06 EST 1998
#
```

## DESCRIPTION

Think of sleep as the snooze alarm of the UNIX world. One personal use of sleep as described next can only begin to attest to its myriad applications.

Say you're forgetful. Your significant other laments this fact and is at wits' end. What do you do? Not to panic. From the command line, type something like:

```
while true
do
    echo  Don't forget paycheck; go home!!!
# substitute banner for echo under drastic circumstances
    sleep 3600
done &
```

You're telling UNIX to repeat a little message on your terminal screen once an hour. Also, the & indicates you want UNIX to run all this in the background so that you can do other things. Don't forget, UNIX is the original multitasking operating system (that is, capable of doing several things at once).

# sort

## FUNCTION
sort lets you sort a single text file, or sort and then merge multiple files.

## GENERAL SYNTAX
```
sort [-c] [-m] [-u] [-o output file] [-ymemory] [-d] [-f]
[-i] [-n] [-r] [input file(s)] [output file]
```

| The parameter . . . | Indicates . . . |
|---|---|
| -c | sort should check to see if its input is sorted; if it is, produce no output, and if it's not, tell you so. Any of the sorting orders can be specified as part of for what it should check. |
| -m | sort should merge its input files. This option assumes that those files are already sorted, and therefore will not sort them. |
| -u | sort should ignore, and not output, duplicate lines. |
| -o output file | sort should write its results to the indicated file, rather than to standard output, as it ordinarily would. sort accepts the same name for both input and output files. |
| -ymemory | the number of kilobytes specified in *memory* should be allocated to sort for its work. |
| -d | sort should work in dictionary mode, that is, it should only sort based on letters, digits, and spaces, ignoring punctuation and other special characters. |
| -f | sort should convert, or as UNIX calls it, *fold*, lowercase letters into uppercase, thereby allowing it to treat words such as buddha, Buddha, and BUDDHA identically. |
| -i | When sorting non-numeric characters, sort should reorder all letters, digits, and punctuation, but not control characters. |
| -n | Sorting should be done numerically, rather than by ASCII or other order. |
| -r | Whatever order sort uses, it should produce output in descending, rather than ascending, sequence. |
| input file(s) | You want to sort these files. |
| output file | This file will contain sorted text. |

## SNEAK PREVIEW

```
# cat 4sort
abc
def
abc
bcd
aaa
# sort -r 4sort
def
bcd
abc
abc
aaa
#
```

## DESCRIPTION

While it asks you to do a little more than simply click an icon or menu item, we'd put the UNIX `sort` command up against any word processor any day. `sort` offers more than enough ways to order text.

## RELATED COMMANDS

comm, diff, uniq

# spell

## FUNCTION
spell checks the correctness of spelling in text files by comparing words from those files to its word list.

## GENERAL SYNTAX
```
spell [-v] [-b] [-x] file(s)
```

| The parameter . . . | Indicates . . . |
|---|---|
| -v | spell should show you all the words it can't find in its list, along with possible alternatives from that list. |
| -b | spell should check against British spelling conventions, such as *colour* and *grey*. |
| -x | spell should show you possible stems for every word it checks. |
| files | You want to spell-check these files. |

## SNEAK PREVIEW
```
# cat 4spell
Tihss file wil containe
several misspelled wurds,
as well as British usage like centre.
# spell 4spell
Tihss
centre
containe
wil
wurds
```

## DESCRIPTION
As you can see from the Sneak Preview, spell excels at finding misspelled words, but does nothing to correct those misspellings. If spell is not installed on your system, try the ispell or ipspell command.

# split

## FUNCTION

split cuts a file horizontally, producing a set of output files, or standard output displays, that are made up of a predefined number of lines.

## GENERAL SYNTAX

```
split [-n] file [outputfile prefix]
```

| The parameter . . . | Indicates . . . |
|---|---|
| -n | split should produce chunks of output of n lines each. If this parameter isn't specified, split assumes you want 1,000-line chunks. |
| file | You want to carve up this file. |
| outputfile prefix | This string will make up the root of the name of every file split creates. For example, if you specify newout for this parameter, and split cuts up its input into five files, these files will be named, respectively, newoutaa, newoutab, newoutac, newoutad, and newoutae. Only if you ask split to create more than 26 output files will this sequence turn over into, for instance, newoutba and so on. |

## SNEAK PREVIEW

```
#
# ls -l 4split*
-rw-rw-rw-   1 root        sys           80 Mar  4 23:56 4split
# cat 4split
This is line 1.
This is line 2.
This is line 3.
This is line 4.
This is line 5
# split -1 4split 4split
# ls -l 4split*
-rw-rw-rw-   1 root        sys           80 Mar  4 23:56 4split
-rw-rw-rw-   1 root        sys           16 Mar  5 00:00 4splitaa
-rw-rw-rw-   1 root        sys           16 Mar  5 00:00 4splitab
-rw-rw-rw-   1 root        sys           16 Mar  5 00:00 4splitac
-rw-rw-rw-   1 root        sys           16 Mar  5 00:00 4splitad
-rw-rw-rw-   1 root        sys           16 Mar  5 00:00 4splitae
#
```

## DESCRIPTION

The maximum total number of files split can produce is 676.

Because of its naming scheme, split requires that any string you supply for the outputfile prefix parameter be at least two characters shorter than the maximum length allowed for a filename on your system.

## RELATED COMMANDS

csplit, cut, join, paste

---

# stty

## FUNCTION
stty sets or displays terminal characteristics.

## GENERAL SYNTAX
    stty [-a] [options]

| The parameter ... | Indicates ... |
|---|---|
| -a | All of the characteristics associated with your current terminal should be described. |
| options | The characteristics you want assigned to your terminal include<br>rows x — Sets the terminal window's number of rows to the value indicated by the parameter x<br>columns x — Sets the terminal window's number of columns to the value indicated by the parameter x<br>parenb — Enables parity checking<br>-parenb — Disables parity checking<br>parodd — Enables odd parity<br>-parodd — Disables odd parity and thereby enables even parity |

## SNEAK PREVIEW

```
#
# stty
speed 9600 baud; evenp hupcl cread
intr = ^C; erase = ^H; kill = ^U;
swtch <undef>;
brkint -inpck icrnl -ixany ixoff onlcr tab3
-iexten echo echoe echok
-echoctl -echoke
#
# stty rows 2
#
```

## DESCRIPTION
Don't precede the option you've chosen with a dash, since stty understands the dash to mean *minus*, that is, disable. Using stty with no options lets you see all your terminal's current operating characteristics. For instance, as the Sneak Preview shows you, the terminal on which we worked with stty was set to communicate at 9,600 baud, use Ctrl+H to erase characters, use Ctrl+C to interrupt execution of the current command, and use Ctrl+U to kill a command.

## RELATED COMMANDS
ps

# sum

## FUNCTION

sum shows you checksums and block counts for files. A *checksum* is a total of the byte values for all individual characters in a file. When this sum is taken and compared to a previous value, the result, if different from that earlier total, can point to possible corruption of the file. A block count, on the other hand, doesn't deal with the correctness of data, but simply with the amount of it, in 512-byte or 1,024-byte chunks, depending on the flavor of UNIX.

## GENERAL SYNTAX

```
sum [-r] file
```

| The parameter . . . | Indicates . . . |
| --- | --- |
| -r | sum should use a different algorithm to calculate checksums. |
| file | You want to check this file's correctness, or size in bytes. |

## SNEAK PREVIEW

```
#
# ls -l core
-rw-------   1 root      sys        1758676 Jan  8 07:55 core
# sum core
40177 3435 core
#
```

## DESCRIPTION

All System V UNIX machines use the same set of algorithms in calculating checksums, which allows you to avoid worrying about the effect of hardware and software versions on the calculation. And as you can see from the Sneak Preview, sum as it's ordinarily used reports both blocks (in the second column of its output) and a checksum automatically. If you do a quick division, you'll also see from this figure that the Hewlett-Packard machine on which it was taken uses 512-byte blocks.

## RELATED COMMANDS

ls, wc

---

# tail

## FUNCTION

`tail`, the mirror image to `head`, lets you grab a specified number of lines from a file. By default, these lines come from the bottom of a file on up. However, with a little extra information supplied, they can come from anywhere in a file. The command sends those lines to any form of output UNIX recognizes.

## GENERAL SYNTAX

```
tail [-b number] [-c number] [-n number or -<#>] file
```

| The parameter ... | Indicates ... |
|---|---|
| `-b number` | The number of 512-byte or 1,024-byte blocks (depending on your flavor of UNIX) `tail` will reproduce from the bottom of a file. |
| `-c number` | The number of bytes the command will reproduce from the bottom of a file. |
| `-n number or -<#>` | The number of lines `tail` will display from the bottom of a file. |
| `file` | The file that `tail` will dissect. If this argument isn't supplied, `tail` will work with standard input. |

## SNEAK PREVIEW

```
# cat testdiff
This is a test file.
#
# tail -c 3 testdiff
e
# tail -b 1 testdiff
This is a test file.
#
```

## DESCRIPTION

Three things about `tail`. First, it stores its results in a 20K buffer. So don't try to use `tail` to reproduce half of the Manhattan phone directory. Second, the command only works on text files. Finally, to get `tail` to stand on its head (groans permitted), enter something like **tail +7-10 somefile**, which will cause `tail` to output lines 7 through 10 of the indicated file, counting from the top, as indicated by the plus sign.

## RELATED COMMANDS

`cat`, `head`, `more`

# tar

## FUNCTION

tar, short for *tape archive*, allows you to create, add to, extract from, or get a listing of, file backups (archives) on any mounted device, not only on tape drives.

## GENERAL SYNTAX

```
tar [function] [mode] [file] [path or file]
```

| The parameter . . . | Indicates . . . |
|---|---|
| function | What you want tar to do, including the following:<br>c — Creates a new archives<br>r — Appends a file or files to the end of the archive<br>u — Adds files to the archive if they're not already there, or if they haven't been modified since the last time the archive was modified<br>t — Takes a table of contents of what's in the archive<br>x — Extracts files from the archive |
| mode | The way in which you wish tar to operate, including the following:<br>v — Tells tar to operate in verbose mode, reporting on every file it processes<br>w — Tells tar to work in confirmation mode, so that it shows you each action it's about to take, and waits for you to tell it whether to proceed, or not<br>f — Tells tar to place the archive in the indicated file rather than to a tape or diskette as it ordinarily would; requires the additional argument file<br>m — Tells tar to forego assigning the modification times of files in its archives to the extracted versions it replaces in the file system, as it ordinarily would, but rather to use the time of extraction as the modification time for extracted files<br>o — Tells tar to assign the user and group ID of the person running the tar command to extracted files, rather than using the files' original IDs |
| file | The name of the file or device on which you wish to create or from which you wish to restore or review an archive |
| path or file | The name of the portion of the file system, or of individual files, which you want to place in, extract from, or check out in the archive |

```
#
# tar -tvf /dev/rmt0
tar: cannot open /dev/rmt0
#
```

## DESCRIPTION

Perhaps the most important thing to note about tar is that its functions, unlike most UNIX commands' options, aren't preceded by a dash. So if you type **tar -t-v -f /dev/rmt0 somefile\*** you may get an error. On the other hand, to create a new archive on the tape drive known to UNIX as /dev/rmt0, and to include all files in the current working directory whose names begin with the string somefile in that archive, you could type **tar cvf /dev/rmt0 somefile\***.

## RELATED COMMANDS

ar, cpio

# tee

## FUNCTION

`tee` creates a double pipeline, so to speak. The output of any commands you pipe to `tee` are placed in a file, as well as simultaneously displayed on standard output.

## GENERAL SYNTAX

```
some command | tee outputfile
```

## SNEAK PREVIEW

```
# cat 4tee
This file will help to demonstrate
the UNIX command tee.
# head -1 4tee | tee fromtee
This file will help to demonstrate
# cat fromtee
This file will help to demonstrate
#
```

## DESCRIPTION

`tee` is one of the handiest of UNIX's many little tools. For instance, it's especially useful when you're developing files or an application; `tee` allows you to eyeball your work and, at the same time, save it for later, more thorough review.

# telnet

## FUNCTION

`telnet`, short for *telephone network*, establishes a connection to a remote host.

## GENERAL SYNTAX

```
telnet host name or host IP address
```

| The parameter ... | Indicates ... |
|---|---|
| host name | The name, as it appears in the UNIX system file /etc/hosts, of the remote machine to which you wish to log in |
| host IP address | The four-part Internet address, of the form 123.45.67.891, which identifies the remote machine to which you wish to connect |

## SNEAK PREVIEW

```
#
# telnet 207.103.236.250
Trying...
Connected to 207.103.236.250.
Escape character is '^]'.
Local flow control on
Telnet TERMINAL-SPEED option ON

HP-UX doli B.10.20 A 9000/816 (ttyp3)

login: lb
Password:
Please wait...checking for disk quotas
```

## DESCRIPTION

`telnet`, like `ftp`, is not one of UNIX's built-in networking commands, but rather is an application, based on the TCP/IP family of protocols, which is available on a wide variety of computer systems. To use `telnet` on any of those systems, you must have a valid user account on the machine to which you're trying to connect.

## RELATED COMMANDS

`ftp`

# test

## FUNCTION

test, used almost exclusively in shell scripts, allows you to examine the nature of files, strings, and numeric expressions.

## GENERAL SYNTAX

```
test file or expression
or
expression
```

| The parameter . . . | Indicates . . . |
| --- | --- |
| file | The file whose nature you want to examine; tests include<br>-r file—See if the indicated file exists and is readable.<br>-w file—See if the indicated file exists and is writeable.<br>-x file—See if the indicated file exists and is executable.<br>-f file—See if the indicated file exists and is an ordinary file (as opposed to, say, a directory or a character-special file).<br>-d file—See if the indicated file exists and is a directory.<br>-c file—See if the indicated file exists and is a character-special file.<br>-b file—See if the indicated file exists and is a block-special file. |
| (string) expression | The string expression whose makeup you want to explore; tests include<br>-z string—See if the indicated string has zero length.<br>-n string—See if the indicated string has nonzero length.<br>-string1 = string2—See if the indicated strings are identical (requires blanks around the equal sign).<br>-string1 != string2—See if the indicated strings are not identical (requires blanks around the inequality operator != ). |
| (numeric) expression | The numeric expression whose nature you want to test; tests include<br>num1 -eq num2—Find out whether num1 is numerically equal to num2. Under this test, the decimal numbers shown as 12 and 012 would pass the test.<br>num1 -ne num2—Find out whether num1 is numerically unequal to num2.<br>num1 -lt num2—Find out whether num1 is numerically less than num2. |

*Continued*

| The parameter . . . | Indicates . . . |
|---|---|
| (numeric) expression | num1 -gt num2 — Find out whether num1 is numerically greater than num2.<br>num1 -le num2 — Find out whether num1 is numerically less than or equal to num2.<br>num1 -ge num2 — Find out whether num1 is numerically greater than or equal to num2. |

## SNEAK PREVIEW

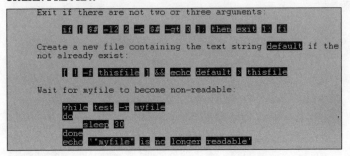

## DESCRIPTION

test is another of those commands most often found in shell scripts. But we think you can see from the Sneak Preview, which offers three examples of using test taken straight from the HP-UX man pages, that test allows you to do some fairly sophisticated scripting.

## RELATED COMMANDS

sh, true

# touch

## FUNCTION

touch updates file access and modification times, even creating an empty file if the one whose name you supply it doesn't exist.

## GENERAL SYNTAX

    touch [-a] [-m] [-c] [mmddhhmimiyy] file(s)

| The parameter ... | Indicates ... |
|---|---|
| -a | touch should update only access time. |
| -m | touch should update only modification time. |
| -c | touch should not create a file if you supply it one that doesn't exist as an argument. |
| mmddhhmimiyy | touch should use the indicated month, day, hour, minute, and year to update the file or files. |
| file(s) | You want to update access or modification times for this file or files. |

## SNEAK PREVIEW

```
# ls -l 4touch
-rw-rw-rw-   1 root         sys            88 Mar  5 00:41 4touch
# touch -t 9910060203.00 4touch
# ls -l 4touch
-rw-rw-rw-   1 root         sys            88 Oct  6 1999 4touch
#
```

## DESCRIPTION

If you use touch without any options, it will update both access and modification times. However you use it, touch is handy for tasks such as keeping files from being automatically archived or removed by shell scripts that check file access or modification times. And as the Sneak Preview shows, you can even specify seconds in supplying dates and times to touch.

## RELATED COMMANDS

ls

# true

## FUNCTION
true lets you report a command exit status of zero; in other words, true gives you the means of simulating successful execution of a command.

## GENERAL SYNTAX
    true

## DESCRIPTION
No Sneak Preview here. Like false and test, true occurs almost exclusively in shell scripts. And remember — however you use true, it will always return a zero value (indicating successful completion); that's its whole reason for being. Using true in a shell script would go something like this:

```
if false
#here, false is just a placeholder
#which indicates that some test has failed
then
     echo Red Alert
#notify the user of the failure, but ...
     true
#simulate successful execution, and then ...
     exit
#just go back to where you started, as if nothing
#unusual had happened
fi
```

## RELATED COMMANDS
false, sh, test

# tty

## FUNCTION

tty tells you the name of the terminal that you're logged in to, as that name appears in UNIX's system files.

## GENERAL SYNTAX

```
tty [-s]
```

| The parameter . . . | Indicates . . . |
|---|---|
| -s | tty should operate in silent mode, not displaying the terminal name. This option is used only in shell scripts that seek to test for the presence or absence of a particular terminal name, by testing for error codes from tty. |

## SNEAK PREVIEW

```
#
# tty
/dev/ttyp3
#
```

## DESCRIPTION

Plain and simple, tty tells you nothing about your terminal's operating characteristics. It just tells you the terminal name.

## RELATED COMMANDS

stty, who

# umask

## FUNCTION

umask reports or changes file creation modes called *masks*.

## GENERAL SYNTAX

```
umask [three-digit octal number]
```

| The parameter . . . | Indicates . . . |
|---|---|
| octal number | The set of permissions with which files have been or will be created. The members of this set are<br>■ column 1, representing file owner permissions<br>■ column 2, representing group permissions<br>■ column 3, representing other user permissions<br>Any of these three columns can have any of the values 0, 1, 2, or 4. These values represent, respectively,<br>    0 — Permissions unchanged from the default<br>    1 — Execute permission<br>    2 — Write permission<br>    3 — Read permission<br>Combine these values to indicate multiple permissions with a single digit. |

## SNEAK PREVIEW

```
#
# umask 006
#
# umask
06
#
```

## DESCRIPTION

To ensure that any files created in the current path, after you run the command, will deny write and execute permission to everyone except the files' owners, you could type **umask 066** as we did in the Sneak Preview. The Sneak Preview also illustrates that using umask with no options displays the current file creation mask.

## RELATED COMMANDS

chmod, ls

# uname

## FUNCTION

uname tells you the type and version of UNIX that's running.

## GENERAL SYNTAX

uname [-s] [-n] [-m] [-v] [-r] [-a]

| The parameter . . . | Indicates . . . |
|---|---|
| -s | uname should display the system name of the machine you're working on. |
| -n | uname should show you the node name, if any, of the machine on which you're working. |
| -m | uname should present the name of the hardware in the machine to which you're connected. |
| -v | uname should tell you what the version of the operating system is. |
| -r | uname should tell you what the release number of the operating system is. |
| -a | You'll see all the information uname has to offer. |

## SNEAK PREVIEW

```
#
# uname -s -r -v
HP-UX B.10.20 A
#
```

## DESCRIPTION

Short and sweet — that's uname. Even with options attached, it's one of the simplest UNIX commands. For example, as you can see from the Sneak Preview, we used uname to discover that we were talking to Hewlett-Packard UNIX release B.10.2, version A.

# uniq

## FUNCTION

uniq finds and removes duplicate lines from a file, if those lines are adjacent.

## GENERAL SYNTAX

```
uniq [-u] [-d] [-c] [-n] [+n] input file [output file]
```

| The parameter | Indicates |
|---|---|
| -u | uniq should create output that contains only lines that are not repeated. |
| -d | uniq should present only one copy of every duplicate line. |
| -c | uniq should prefix each line of output with a count of how many times the line was found in the input file. |
| -n | uniq should ignore the number of fields in adjacent lines represented by n when looking for duplicates. |
| +n | uniq should ignore the first n number of characters when searching for duplicates. |
| input file | You want to search for duplicate lines in this file. |
| output file | You want uniq to place its output into this file. |

## SNEAK PREVIEW

```
#
# cat testdigg
This is a test file.
This is not a test file.
This is another line.
This is another line.
This is not another duplicate line.

# uniq testdigg fromuniq
# cat fromuniq
This is a test file.
This is not a test file.
This is another line.
This is not another duplicate line.
#
```

## DESCRIPTION

If you supply no output filename to uniq, it will write its results to standard output. But if you try to use the same filename for both input and output, uniq may fail.

## RELATED COMMANDS

cmp, diff, wc

---

# unpack

## FUNCTION

unpack decompresses files that have been compressed with pack.

## GENERAL SYNTAX

```
unpack file(s)
```

| The parameter . . . | Indicates . . . |
|---|---|
| file(s) | The files you want unpack to decompress |

## SNEAK PREVIEW

```
#
# pack core
pack: core: 52.2% Compression
# ls *.z
core.z
# unpack core.z
unpack: core: unpacked
# ls *.z
*.z not found
# pack core
pack: core: 52.2% Compression
# ls *.z
core.z
# unpack core
unpack: core: unpacked
# ls *.z
*.z not found
#
```

## DESCRIPTION

As the Sneak Preview shows, you can specify the file you want unpack to decompress in either of two ways. If your system uses the compress command, use uncompress; if your system uses the gzip command, use gunzip. You can recognize files compressed with the compress command by their .Z extension; files compressed with gzip have a .gz extension.

## RELATED COMMANDS

pack, pcat (plus compress, uncompress, zcat, gzip, and gunzip on some systems)

---

# uux

## FUNCTION
One of the family of built-in networking commands UNIX offers, uux lets you execute commands on a remote UNIX system without having to connect to that system. Like its siblings, uux takes care of all intersystem communications for you.

## GENERAL SYNTAX
```
uux [ j, n, a<username>, b, c, C, r, s<filename>, z]
command or script name
```

| The parameter . . . | Indicates . . . |
|---|---|
| -j | UNIX and uux should use standard input for the commands you want it to carry out on the remote system. |
| n | UNIX should *not* tell you if uux fails to do what you ask. |
| a username | when uux runs on the remote host, you'll be identified there by the user name specified in the username field, rather than by your user ID number. |
| b | if uux fails, what you told it to do will be echoed back to you. |
| c | uux should forego its normal practice of copying the file named in the command line to the UNIX spool directory as preparation for transferring the file. |
| C | uux will be forced to copy the file named in the command line to the UNIX spool directory as preparation for transferring the file. |
| r | UNIX and the remote host should queue the task you've asked to carry out, but not begin file transfers right away. |
| sfilename | uux should let you know the transfer status of the file you've specified in the filename portion of this parameter. Unlike the a option, s and filename must have no spaces between them. |
| z | uux should tell you that it's succeeded in doing what you asked on the remote host. |
| command or script name | The name of the shell command or shell script you want to execute on the remote host. |

## SNEAK PREVIEW

```
uux -n cat nonexistantfile
```

## DESCRIPTION

You could use `uux` to browse through the file system of a remote UNIX machine. Here's how one such scanning session might go:

```
uux "martial_arts!ls -l /usr/master/tips > kungfu
```

This command produces a full listing of all unhidden files in the directory `/usr/master/tips` on the machine known as `martial_arts` and appends the results of running the command to a file called `kungfu` on your UNIX computer.

In order to use `uux` successfully, the host on which you try to execute a command must be recognized by your local system, usually in the file `/etc/hosts`. As you can see if you scan the command line given here, the name of the command or script you want to carry out should be prefixed by a string that contains the remote host's name and an exclamation point (!). If you don't supply this prefix, some versions of UNIX may think you want to carry out the command locally.

## RELATED COMMANDS

cu, uucp

---

# vi

**FUNCTION**

vi is the UNIX line-oriented text editor.

**GENERAL SYNTAX**

```
vi [moving around in a file] [inserting, replacing,
and removing text] [quitting, saving, and viewing]
```

| The parameter . . . | Includes and indicates . . . |
|---|---|
| moving around in a file | The keystrokes or keystroke combinations you must use to move back and forth through the text you're creating and editing; some of the most frequently used of these are as follows (note the case of each combination): |
| | The up, down, right, and left arrow keys — Each single press of one of these keys moves you a single character position in the indicated direction. |
| | j — Moves the cursor one character position up. |
| | k — Moves the cursor one character position down. |
| | h — Moves the cursor one character to the left. |
| | l — One of UNIX's few un-mnemonic indicators, moves the cursor one character to the right. |
| | +some number, or -some number — Moves you forward or back respectively some number of lines in a file from the current cursor position. |
| | w — Moves you forward through the text you're working with, one word at a time, to the beginning of the next word. To vi, a word is almost always set off by blanks or tabs. |
| | b — Moves you backwards through the text you're working with, one word at a time, to the beginning of the previous word. |
| | e — Moves you forward through the text you're working with, to the end of the next word. |
| | 0, (zero) — Moves you to the beginning of the current line. |
| | $ — Moves you to the end of the current line, no matter how many times that line has wrapped. |
| | G — Moves you to the end, or ground, of a file. |
| | G plus some number — Moves you to the line in the file indicated by the number you type. (7+Shift+G, for instance, would place the cursor at the seventh line of a file.) |

| The parameter . . . | Includes and indicates . . . |
| --- | --- |
| inserting, replacing, and removing text | Press Esc to tell vi that you're done entering text. But you need not do so to tell the editor you're done deleting, pasting, or replacing.<br><br>i — Inserts text to the left of the cursor.<br>I — Inserts text at the beginning of the current line.<br>a — Appends text, that is, place new text to the right of the cursor position, even if that position is at the end of a line.<br>o — Opens a new, blank line below the current line.<br>0 — Opens a new, blank line above the current line.<br>y — Yanks, that is cut, the highlighted text.<br>Y — Yanks the current line.<br>p — Places deleted or cut text or lines below the current line.<br>P — Places deleted or cut text or lines above the current line.<br>dd — Deletes the current line; may be accompanied by a repeat parameter, such as 7. (So keying **7dd** would cause vi to delete seven lines, starting with the current line.)<br>d — Deletes the highlighted text.<br>D — Deletes all text from the current cursor position to the end of the current line.<br>dw — Deletes the current word; like dd, can be accompanied by a repeat parameter.<br>cw — Changes the current word. (Typing **cw** causes a $ character to be placed at the end of the current word, as vi's signal to you that you can begin entering your changes.)<br>x — Deletes the single character at the current cursor position.<br>r — Replaces the single character at the current cursor position. |
| quitting, saving, and viewing | q! — Quits a vi session immediately, without saving any changes<br>qall! — Quits a session without saving changes, but not as quickly as :q!<br>:w — Writes, that is, saves, to the file changes you've made up to that point, but to keep your session active.<br>:wq — Writes your changes and then end your session.<br>:se nu — Causes vi to display line numbers for the file you're working on.<br>:se nonu — Removes line numbers from the display of a file. |

## DESCRIPTION

Entire books have been written about vi. We're partial to one called *Learning the vi Editor*, published by O'Reilly and Associates. What we've presented here may be only a few pages. But it's enough to get you started with creating and modifying files.

# wait

## FUNCTION

`wait` causes UNIX to delay reactivating the shell until any and all background processes that might be running have completed. Or, you can use `wait` more discriminatingly. If you supply it with a process ID number, `wait` instructs UNIX to cool it only until the background process that ID indicates is done running.

## GENERAL SYNTAX

```
wait [PID]
```

| The parameter . . . | Indicates . . . |
|---------------------|-----------------|
| PID | The ID number of the process for whose completion UNIX will wait before going back simply to executing a shell session |

## SNEAK PREVIEW

```
# cat trek_triv
federashun
space
frontier
# cat 4wait
spell trek_triv > ok_triv&
wait
cat ok_triv
# ./4wait
federashun
#
```

## DESCRIPTION

`wait` is often used to delay execution of a command, in order to give it time to run to completion before it passes its results to another command. For example, if you've created a file in `vi` that you want to spell-check, you could do that and see the corrected results by using this little shell script:

```
spell trek_triv > ok_triv  &
wait
cat ok_triv
```

The script's first line does the hard work, but it does it in the background. Its second line forces UNIX to wait until that check is complete before using `cat` to show you the final results.

## RELATED COMMANDS

`kill`, `sh`, `sleep`

# wall

## FUNCTION

wall *(write to all users)*, like write, lets you send e-mail-like, noninteractive messages to users logged in to your system. Unlike write, though, wall doesn't ask you to specify where users might be UNIXing from. That's because wall *broadcasts* its messages. That is, it sends a separate copy of whatever you type to every user logged in to your system.

## GENERAL SYNTAX

    wall

Or, on some systems:

    /etc/wall

This applies in a general sense to all systems.

## SNEAK PREVIEW

```
#
# wall
HELLO, EVERYONE!

Broadcast Message from root (ttyp4) Tue Mar  3 00:54:56...
HELLO, EVERYONE!
#
```

## DESCRIPTION

Let's say you're logged in to your system's console, as the user root. Keying in **wall**, pressing Enter, typing **HELLO, EVERYONE!**, pressing Enter, and pressing Ctrl+D produces a display like the following on the screen of every user, including you, who's currently logged in to your machine.

    Broadcast message from root
    HELLO, EVERYONE!

## RELATED COMMANDS

echo, write

---

# WC

## FUNCTION
wc, which stands for *word count*, counts words, characters, or lines (usually in files) and reports its tally to you.

## GENERAL SYNTAX
```
wc [lwc] [files]
```

| The parameter ... | Indicates ... |
|---|---|
| lwc | The options l for lines, w for words, or c for characters define what you want wc to count. You can use any, any combination of, all, or none of these options if you need. |
| files | The files that you want wc to examine. If you don't supply this argument, wc checks out standard input. |

## SNEAK PREVIEW
```
#
# ls -l buzz-builder
-rwx------    1 root           sys           1547
# wc -l buzz-builder
50 buzz-builder
# wc -w buzz-builder
186 buzz-builder
# wc -c buzz-builder
1547 buzz-builder
# wc buzz-builder
50 186 1547 buzz-builder
#
```

## DESCRIPTION
As you can see from the Sneak Preview, supplying no options to wc causes it to count everything it understands, while supplying specific options to it causes it to report its findings in the order in which you supplied the options.

## RELATED COMMANDS
ls

# who

## FUNCTION

who lets you do the following things:

- Find out what users are currently logged in to your system
- Find out the user name under which you yourself logged in

## GENERAL SYNTAX

```
who [u, T, I, H, q, p, d, b, a] [alternate sourcefile]
```

| The parameter . . . | Indicates . . . |
|---|---|
| u | UNIX should tell you only about those users currently logged in. |
| T | UNIX should tell you the *state* of the terminal to which a user is logged in, that is, if you can write to that terminal. |
| I | UNIX should tell you only about those connections, lines, or devices where a login attempt is taking place. |
| H | UNIX should place headers at the beginning of each column of output you see. |
| q | UNIX should tell you only the names and terminal numbers of logged-in users, and omit the third default parameter who would otherwise supply: the time the user logged in (q stands for a *quick* output). |
| p | UNIX should tell you about more than just logged-in users — it should tell you about any active processes started by the system-level command init. Why this mix-and-match output? Because UNIX and who consider logins as processes. |
| d | UNIX should tell you about processes that have died (literally, processes that have outlived their allotted execution time). |
| b | UNIX should tell you about the time and date the system was most recently rebooted. |
| a | UNIX should use all options in this table to who except q. |
| alternate sourcefile | UNIX should use the indicated file rather than the file /etc/utmp, which would be who's usual source of information, to respond to your request. |

## SNEAK PREVIEW

```
# who
root        ttyp4       Mar  3 00:07
#
```

---

**DESCRIPTION**

If you've forgotten the user name under which you connected to UNIX, type **who am i**.

You'll see a response something like this:

```
root            console         Dec 12 18:48
```

which tells you that you logged in to UNIX at the system console, at 6:48 PM on December 12, as the user *root*.

Or, simply typing **who** and then pressing Enter presents you with a list of all users currently logged in to the UNIX machine that executes this command.

**RELATED COMMANDS**

mesg, su, talk, tty, wall, write

# write

## FUNCTION

write allows you to send messages, akin to email, to another logged-in user of your system.

## GENERAL SYNTAX

```
write user-id [station id]
```

| The parameter ... | Indicates ... |
|---|---|
| user-id | The user with whom you want to communicate |
| station-id | The terminal number to which that user has logged in |

## SNEAK PREVIEW

```
# write root ttyp3
        Message from root (ttyp3) [ Wed Dec 17 20:03:26 ] ...
I am he as you are me as we are all together ...
I am he as you are me as we are all together ...
<EOT>
#
```

## DESCRIPTION

write is a little picky in how it wants you to begin and end your messages. You must start by keying in a string like **write tb tty110** and pressing Enter.

This string causes the user logged into terminal 110 under the name tb to see the following line on his or her screen:

```
Message from lm (tty99)
```

Meanwhile, back at your terminal (tty99), you type the message you want to send to tb. Then, when you're done, you simply press Ctrl+D to hang up the phone, so to speak; tb saw whatever you typed as soon as you finished keying it in.

## RELATED COMMANDS

banner, echo, mesg, talk, wall, who

# RESOURCES

The two sections in this bibliography respectively contain information on

- print sources of more information on UNIX
- World Wide Web sources of the same

When perusing the second section, remember the volatility of the Web. We checked out every URL here as this book was being written, but the addresses of these pages may have changed by the time the book was printed.

## Print Sources

*Advanced Topics in Unix: Processes, Files, and Systems.* Ronald J. Leach. John Wiley & Sons, 1994.

Extensive coverage of many topics not found elsewhere, including manipulating the UNIX file system, and memory and process management.

*Awk Programming Language, The.* Alfred V. Aho, Brian W. Kernighan, and Peter J. Weinberger. Addison-Wesley, 1988.

Learn more about awk, a really neat little language, from a book written by the three men who created the language.

*Learning the vi Editor, 5th Rev Edition.* O'Reilly & Associates, 1990.

If you've never checked out one of those rather plain-looking, slightly skinny computer reference books with a little animal on the cover, this one from O'Reilly's excellent series would be a good place to start. vi is, like so many things about UNIX, a topic all to itself.

*UNIX Programming for Dummies.* James Edward Keogh, Jim Keogh, and Kathy Ivens. IDG Books Worldwide, 1996.

Explains shell script programming basics and how to use this basic knowledge to customize UNIX.

*UNIX System Security.* Rick Farrow. Addison-Wesley, 1990.

Security is considered by some to be an area in which UNIX can fall short. This book covers what you need to know about UNIX system security.

*Unix System V Bible: Commands and Utilities.* The Waite Group. Sams, 1987.

While this book is currently out of print, you can still find a copy if you try. We consider it one of the best overall UNIX reference books. Our copy has been well used for years.

# Online Sources

We've gathered what we feel to be the most comprehensive and authoritative sites on a few flavors of UNIX.

## Berkeley UNIX

**FreeBSD:** http://www.freebsd.org/

One of the many neat things about UNIX is how many generous people, like those at the FreeBSD organization, work to enhance it, and then give away the results for free.

**BSD Archives:** http://www.leo.org/archiv/bsd/

Another nice thing about UNIX is that it and the folks who work on it have a sense of humor.

## Linux

**Linux Hot Sites:** http://mmm.mbhs.edu/~fwright/hotsites.html

This page offers links to information on some of the most important characteristics of Linux.

**Linux Online:** http://www.linux.org/

Linux Online is the official Linux contributors' group site.

## System V UNIX

**Ulrik Vieth's Hotlist:** http://www.thphy.uni-duesseldorf.de/~vieth/subjects/computer/

As we mention earlier, legions of folks all around the world contribute to UNIX. Ulrich Vieth of Dusseldorf, Germany, for instance, put in a lot of time and effort placing a number of important pieces of System V documentation on the Web.

## Vendor-Specific Versions of UNIX

**Digital Equipment Corporation:** http://www.unix.digital.com/

DIGITAL UNIX (when you're talking about the operating system rather than just the company, the caps are appropriate) has a neat twist — a built-in ability to interface with Windows NT.

**Hewlett-Packard:** http://www.hp.com/computing/next_genunix/main.html

Hewlett-Packard takes UNIX seriously.

# GLOSSARY

**8-bit clean** A system that supports a standard method of representing characters in the various European languages, and which uses 8-bit character sets; for example ISO Latin 1.

**abort** To prematurely, but in a controlled manner, terminate a computer process.

**absolute path name** The complete list of the directories and subdirectories that lie between a file and the root directory, components of which are separated by a slash character (/).

**access** To locate a file or device, read it into memory, and make it ready for processing.

**acknowledge character (ACK)** A transmission control character that signifies an affirmative response; most frequently pertains to data communications.

**address** Either a hexadecimal number used by an operating system to identify a storage location in memory, or in data communications, a unique code that identifies a station on a network.

**address space** A range of memory locations in which a CPU can store management information on all of the memory where available.

**allocate** To set aside memory for a program or program module; can be static or dynamic.

**American Standard Code for Information Interchange (ASCII)** A very widely used form of binary encoding of characters that uses seven bits to represent data, and an eighth bit to indicate the beginning or end of a byte.

**append** To place at the end of; most frequently used in the context of writing to a file.

**archive** A single file made up of several files that have been gathered together and identified as a library or archive by a program such as `tar` or `ar`.

**argument** Information supplied to a command which gives the command more detailed instructions. For example, an argument may be the name of a file to be processed, or the type of output the command is to produce.

**assignment operator** Operator that assigns a value to a variable; in awk and shell script programming, the equal sign (=).

**asynchronous** Not based on a coordinated time relationship; unpredictable in the context of the execution of a program's instructions; in data communications, sending one character at a time, with varying intervals between characters, and therefore requiring start and stop bits.

**background process** A command that the system works on in such a way as to allow other commands to continue to be submitted to the command interpreter; UNIX interprets the ampersand character (&), placed at the end of a command, as meaning that the command should run in the background.

**backup** A copy on any of a variety of storage media of important information. Under UNIX, backups are most often produced by `tar` or `cpio`.

**baud rate** Rate at which data is transferred between devices; *not* exactly equivalent to bits per second. Baud rate measures the number of events, or changes in the nature of a signal, that occur in 1 second; one such event can encode more than one bit. So, a 9,600 "baud" modem that encodes four bits per event actually operates at 2,400 baud but transmits 9,600 bits per second (2,400 events times four bits per event).

**Berkeley Software Distribution (BSD)** A family of versions of UNIX developed at the University of California, Berkeley.

**binary** Referring to the base-2 number system, in which values are expressed as combinations of two digits, *0* and *1*, the only symbols available under this system. For example, the number we know, in decimal notation, as *8* is represented in binary as 1,000 (no *1*'s, no *2*'s, no *4*'s, but a single *8*).

**bit (*binary digit*)** Smallest unit of information a computer can handle; can have only one of two possible values: *1* (on) or *0* (off).

**bit bucket** UNIX slang for `/dev/null`, or the *null device*. Think of it as a black hole from which no data emerges.

**bitwise operator** Also called *unary operator*. An operator that evaluates the Boolean conditions AND, OR, or NOT, requiring only one operand, and resulting in a TRUE or FALSE value.

**block** A unit of data storage of predefined size. Under most versions of UNIX currently in use, 1,024 bytes.

**block device** A storage medium, such as a hard drive or CD-ROM drive, from and to which transfers of entire blocks of data at a single time are possible.

**Boolean** Logical or true/false values or operations.

**browse** To scan data such as a list of files without changing any information.

**buffer** A temporary work or storage area in memory or on disk; if the latter, it attempts to mimic memory. Commonly used by programs such as editors that carry out a high percentage of data modification.

**bug** An error or inaccuracy in hardware or software.

**byte** A group of adjacent bits which, taken as a whole, represent what to us would be one character. The number of bits needed to make up a byte varies according to the encoding method used.

**byte order** Order in which bytes are stored in memory; hardware-specific.

**cache** A buffer of high-speed memory, filled at medium speed from main memory, which often holds frequently executed program instructions. Helps increase effective processor speed.

**call** To temporarily transfer execution control to another program or subprogram.

**case sensitive** Able, as UNIX is, to distinguish between uppercase and lowercase letters.

**CCITT (Comite Consultatif Internationale de Telegraphie et Telephonie)** Part of the United Nations *International Telecommunications Union* (ITU). Based in Geneva, Switzerland, CCITT recommends communications standards such as networking protocols.

**chaining** Linking two or more entities so they are dependent upon one another for operation; can be applied to program modules, data storage media, or data communications devices.

**change mode** Changing the parameters that define who may use a file, and for what purpose; under UNIX, done with the command chmod.

**character** Symbol that represents a letter, number, punctuation, or control character; that is, data that is merely representative, and upon which no calculations can be carried out.

**character device** Computer component that receives or transmits data as a stream of characters, one at a time. Compare to block device.

**character set** Alphabetical, numeric, and other characters that have something, such as their encoding method, in common; for instance, the ASCII character set, made up of letters, numbers, symbols, and control codes.

**child directory** A subdirectory.

**child process** A process created dynamically by another process, the latter known as the *parent process*.

**client/server** A model for networking and the programs distributed by networks under which a machine such as a PC or terminal requests services from another, more powerful machine such as a minicomputer. For example, the UNIX and Internet Domain Name System (DNS) and Network File System (NFS).

**command** An instruction to a computer; usually presented to the machine as a character string.

**command interpreter** A form of user/computer interface that accepts commands from the keyboard and passes the commands to the operating system kernel, where they are executed; in UNIX, can be C shell, Bourne shell, or others.

**command line** Under UNIX, a string of characters that represents a command and any arguments, options, or other parameters that may be required by, or supplied at the user's discretion to, the command; must be terminated by the end-of-line character, in order to tell UNIX that you've given it all the information needed for the current execution of the command.

**command prompt** Character or string of characters displayed to tell a user the operating system is ready to accept and interpret the next command line; under UNIX, frequently the dollar sign ($) character for most users, and the pound sign (#) character for the superuser.

**concatenate** To string together two or more sequences into one longer sequence, as in, for example, using the UNIX command `cat` to string files together.

**concurrent** A condition under which two or more computer processes may simultaneously access the CPU and are therefore carried out more or less simultaneously.

**conditional** Action or operation that takes place only if a particular condition is true.

**control character** Characters such as Ctrl+D, typed by pressing a key while the Ctrl key is held down, which have special meaning to an operating system. For example, Ctrl+C tells UNIX to end a process.

**core file or core dump** A file, created when a program malfunctions and crashes, which holds a snapshot of what was in memory at the moment of the crash. Can be used as a debugging tool.

**crash** To fail suddenly and often cataclysmically.

**cron** UNIX daemon that executes commands at specified dates and times.

**crontab file** Lists commands to be executed at specified dates and times by `cron`.

**C shell** The standard Berkeley UNIX shell.

**curly brace** The bracket characters { and } frequently used as delimiters by UNIX and C.

**current directory** Directory at the end of a path, searched first for files and programs, and the one in which new information will be stored unless you tell UNIX otherwise.

**daemon** A background process that typically carries out commands delivered for remote execution, such as e-mail, handled by the mailer daemon, or printing, handled by the printer daemon.

**decimal** Base-10 numbering system that uses the ten digits 0 through 9. Compare to octal or base-8, which uses the eight digits 0 through 7; binary or base-2, which uses only the digits 0 and 1; or hexadecimal or base -6, which uses not only the digits 0 through 9 but also the letters A through F. The more symbols that are available to a numbering system, the more compactly it can represent data. For example, binary notation requires four digits to represent the value 10 (1010), decimal notation requires two (10), and hexadecimal notation only needs one (A).

**delimiter** A character that separates and organizes data. Under UNIX these can be the square brackets [ ], the parentheses ( ), or the curly braces { }. White space such as blanks and tabs can also act as delimiters.

**demand paging** A technique under which the memory set aside for a program is noncontiguous, that is, isn't made up of adjacent sections, and under which parts of the program are shifted in and out of memory, allowing an operating system that uses it (such as UNIX) to execute programs that are larger than the available physical memory.

**device driver** Software that controls devices such as modems, graphics adapters, hard drives, CD-ROM drives, and so on.

**device name** Used by UNIX to identify component devices such as drives; for example, /dev/rst0, used by many UNIX systems to represent a 1/4-inch tape drive.

**directory** A file that contains location and content information about actual data files.

**directory stack** A stack or memory buffer in the C shell that allows users to save frequently used directories and then quickly jump from one directory to another; manipulated by the built-in C shell command pushd, which places the directory on the stack; popd, which removes or pops the top entry from the stack; dirs, which displays a list of directories currently on the stack.

**disk quotas** Technique used to control which of a file system's resources a user can access. Under most versions of UNIX, disk quotas are optional and must be specifically configured by a system administrator.

**driver/kernel interface (DKI)** Interface between the UNIX operating system kernel and drivers; a set of driver-defined functions that are called by the kernel, and which act as entry points into a driver.

**dynamic allocation** Technique under which system resources assigned to a process are determined at the moment of need.

**dynamic RAM (DRAM**; pronounced *dee-ram*) Type of random-access memory that stores information in integrated circuits that contain components called capacitors. Capacitors lose their charge over time, so DRAM must be refreshed periodically.

**echo** To repeat a stream of characters, most frequently sent to a monitor.

**embedded** Entities like program code or commands that are built into a more inclusive entity rather than being called by the latter entity.

**encryption** Making information unintelligible or indecipherable, in order to protect it from unauthorized viewing or use, usually involves a key without which the information cannot be decoded or decrypted.

**end-of-file (EOF)** The key combination, usually Ctrl+D in UNIX, that tells an operating system it has reached the end of a body of data such as a file.

**environment** Conditions under which a user works with an operating system; includes parameters like the shell prompt, the user's home directory, the user's login name and password, the type of terminal a user is working from (for instance, VT220), specifics for backspace and erase characters, and so on.

**environment variable** UNIX shell variables that identify specifics about a user's environment.

**errno** UNIX colloquialism for the concept or term *error number*.

**escape** To cause UNIX to ignore, that is to forego executing, any meaning attached to special characters such as the ampersand (&) or pipe symbol (|); done by preceding the character in question with a \ character.

**Ethernet** A type of network and data communications medium developed by Xerox in 1976 and standardized by the Institute of Electrical and Electronics Engineers (IEEE) in its 802.x standards. Thin Ethernet cabling is 5 millimeters in diameter and can connect stations over a distance of 300 meters. Thick Ethernet cabling is 1 centimeter in diameter and can connect stations up to 1,000 meters apart.

**event processing** In advanced operating systems such as UNIX, the ability to create and maintain a queue for processing system- and user-initiated events.

**executable** A file that can be executed by a computer without any translation, that is, a compiled or interpreted binary file.

**execute** To run a program, or to carry out program instructions.

**execution time** Number of ticks of the system clock — that is, pulses of a computer's internal timer — that a CPU needs to decode and carry out an instruction after that instruction has been fetched from memory; the second half of an instruction cycle, the first half being taken by fetching the instruction.

**extension** That portion of a filename, occurring after the dot (.) character, which indicates the type of file. Unlike some other operating systems, UNIX can accept filename extensions longer than three characters.

**fatal error** One that causes an application or entire system to crash.

**field** To UNIX, a subsection of a string.

**file** A complete, named collection of logically related data.

**file format** Internal structuring that specifies how a file is stored and displayed.

**filename expansion** Process through which UNIX matches filenames containing metacharacters to actual filenames. For instance, matching `foo?` to `foo`, `foot`, `food`, and `fool`.

---

**file permissions** Parameters that are assigned to every UNIX file and directory, and that specify who may use those files and directories, and for what purpose. Purposes may be read (display), write (modify or transfer), and execute.

**first-in, first-out (FIFO)** Processing a queue in such a way that items are removed in the order in which they were added — the first in is also the first out. A print queue is an example of a FIFO process.

**flag** Command argument or modifier, usually preceded on the command line by a hyphen ( - ).

**flavor** Data-processing slang for a category or type of software. In UNIX, common flavors are System V and Berkeley.

**flush** To clear an area of memory.

**foreground** Running under direct control of a user or terminal; thereby preventing the terminal from being used for anything else until the foreground task finishes running.

**fork** System call or execution of instruction, which creates a new process called a *child process.*

**fragmentation** Refers to the practice of some operating systems of scattering parts of the same file across various areas of a hard disk, thereby increasing access and retrieval time, and possibly eventually causing physical damage to the disk drive. UNIX incurs little or no fragmentation, since by default it stores all portions of a file contiguously, that is, next to one another.

**gigabyte (Gbyte** or **GB)** Exactly 1,073,741,824 bytes (approximately 1 billion bytes).

**global** Having extended or general scope. For example, a global substitution of one word for another in a file affects all occurrences of the original word.

**group** A collection of users who can be referred to by a common name. The group to which a user belongs affects his or her access to files.

**group ID (GID)** Identification number for a group.

**halt** To intentionally and — one hopes, in an orderly fashion — stop a system.

**handler** Software module that carries out common and/or simple tasks such as accepting input or displaying error messages.

**hard link** Directory-file entry that specifically refers to a disk file. There may be more than one hard link to a given file under UNIX. For example, the single physical file jackiechan may be listed in the directory file of both the kungfu and the acrobatics directories.

**hexadecimal** Base-16 numbering.

**hidden character** Any character in the standard ASCII set that is not printable.

**hidden file** Special type of UNIX file that isn't displayed by normal file listings; for example, .login or .profile.

---

**home directory** Directory into which a user is placed upon login.

**hung** A condition in which the system does not respond to commands.

**idle** The time during, or the condition of, a device being operational but not in use.

**initialization files** Files in a user's home directory whose names are prefixed with the dot (.) character, and which set a number of environment variables such as default path.

**init states** Initialization states, that is, levels at which a UNIX system can run; for example, single-user.

**inode** An entry in a UNIX system table, called the inode table or inode file; describes where a file is located on a drive, the file's size, when it was last used, and so on — all the information supplied to and by the command `ls`.

**inode table/file** Under UNIX, the analog to a DOS or Windows directory file.

**input stream** A sequence of bytes that act as raw material for a process; for example, a series of characters read from the keyboard into memory.

**instruction stream** A serially executed set of instructions.

**instruction time** Also called fetch time; number of clock ticks needed to retrieve an instruction from memory.

**interprocess control (IPC)** Coordinating the sharing of data between two or more processes.

**interrupt** To break off executing a command or other process; also, the signal that causes this breaking-off.

**interrupt handler** Software routine executed when a specific interrupt occurs. Different interrupts have different handlers.

**ioctl (input/output or I/O control)** Software that controls the functioning of storage devices and the placement or retrieval of data to or from them.

**iteration** Carrying out an instruction or series of instructions repeatedly; that is, looping.

**job** Processing performed as a unit by a computer.

**job (process) number** Identification number assigned to each process running on a computer.

**kernel** The core of an operating system; manages hardware and supplies basic services such as the file system.

**kernel architecture** The way in which an operating system kernel is built; for example, 32-bit or 64-bit architectures.

**kill** Explicitly terminating a process before it can run to completion.

**link** Entry in a directory file that links a user-assigned name for a file to the system's identification number for that file; under UNIX, can be *hard* or *symbolic*.

---

**linker** Software module that links compiled programs with data files to create an executable.

**literal** A value, most frequently encased in double quotes under UNIX, which represents nothing but itself; for example, `"123"`.

**local** Limited scope or effect, as in a local variable or a local process.

**login shell** The default shell to which a user logs in.

**magic number** A numeric constant that indicates file type.

**man pages** Online UNIX documentation; can be cryptic.

**megabyte (Mbyte or MB)** Exactly 1,048,576 bytes or 1,024 kilobytes; approximately 1 million bytes.

**message** Software-generated information that tells users about the status of a process.

**metacharacter** A character with some special meaning; under UNIX, includes, among others, the ampersand (&), the pound sign (#), the asterisk (*), and the question mark (?), the last of which UNIX interprets as a place-holder for any single character.

**megahertz (MHz)** One million cycles per second of an electromagnetic signal.

**mode** Operational condition of a computer or program.

**mount** Associating a directory or subdirectory name with a physical storage device.

**mount point** A directory on one computer to which you mount a file system that exists on a remote computer.

**move** Transferring information from one location to another; unlike a copy, which duplicates information.

**multitasking** The concurrent execution of two or more tasks by a computer.

**multiuser** A computer system or operational mode that can be used concurrently by more than one person.

**named pipe** A FIFO file that can be used as a pipe by a System V process.

**negative acknowledge (NAK)** Special character that indicates failure to complete a process or receive data.

**nibble** Half a byte (generally, four bits).

**nice value** Number representing the priority level of a UNIX process, with *0* being the usual default priority, and *20* being the *lowest* priority (the higher the number, the slower the process runs); appears under the header `NI` in some forms of the process status (`ps`) command; can be manipulated by the command `nice`.

**null character** An invisible character with an internal code of 0 that occupies no space if printed. Not to be confused with a blank, which is invisible but occupies a space.

**null string**  String that holds no characters; that is, one whose length is zero.

**object file**  File containing machine language code; that is, an executable file.

**octal**  Base-8 number system, which uses only the digits 0 through 7; used in software as a compact means of representing binary numbers, which are commonly divided into groups of three bits for conversion to octal.

**octet**  A byte composed of eight bits.

**path**  The description of the spot occupied by a file within a file system; includes any directories and subdirectories that intervene between the file and the root of the file system.

**permission**  The ability of a user to perform a particular operation on a file; under UNIX, can be read, write, or execute.

**pipe**  Connecting two commands, so that the output of the first becomes the input of the second.

**priority**  Level of importance or immediacy assigned to a process; higher-priority processes, indicated by smaller integers under UNIX, will execute before lower-priority ones.

**queue**  A waiting line in memory into which data needed for processes is placed.

**raw**  Without formatting, as in a raw device, that is, a character device — one that simply transfers a data stream.

**redirect**  To cause input to be taken from, or output to be sent to, a location other than the default; under UNIX, redirecting input is indicated by the less-than or left-pointing angle bracket (<), while redirecting output is indicated by the greater-than or right-pointing angle bracket (>).

**remote**  Taking place or being located at a distant spot, as in *remote host*.

**sleep**  Suspending processing for a predefined period of time; unlike wait, does not require the completion of another process in order to end.

**stack**  A waiting line in memory into which program instructions about to be carried out are placed.

**stall**  Unintentional delay in processing.

**standard error (stderr)**  The UNIX term for a generic file, indicated to and in the shell by the digit 2, which is the default destination for system error messages; usually associated with the monitor.

**standard input (stdin)**  The UNIX term for a generic file, indicated to and in the shell by the digit 0, which is the default source for input; usually associated with the keyboard.

**standard output (stdout)**  The UNIX term for a generic file, indicated to and in the shell by the digit 1, which is the default destination for the output of commands; usually associated with the monitor.

---

**suspend** To temporarily cause an intentional delay in processing; under UNIX, accomplished with either `sleep` or `wait`.

**virtual** Functionally but not physically equivalent to, as in *virtual machine*.

**wait** To require the completion of another process or the reception of data items.

**wait state** Condition in which a computer passively awaits some event such as the click of a mouse or a request for a service from a client.

# INDEX

**NOTE:** Parameters preceded by symbols (such as +, -, or \) are listed by first alphabetic character except for those including numbers. Parameters that use numbers are listed under the heading Numbers.

alphabetic representation
parameter (chmod command),
48
alternate sourcefile parameter
(who command), 153
append indicator (>>), 8, 9, 44
appending files, 43–44
ar command
related commands, 55–56,
133–134
summary of, 36
archive parameter (ar command),
36
archive-key parameter (ar
command), 36
archives. *See* ar command; touch
command
arguments parameter (nohup
command), 106
arguments
entering on command line, 5
setting priorities for, 104–105
ascii parameter (ftp command), 82
at command, related commands,
40, 57
automating shell scripts, 57
awk command, summary of, 37

## B

-b parameter (spell command), 128
-b number parameter (tail
command), 132
\b parameter (echo command),
72–73
b parameter
for uux command, 146

for who command, 153
banner command, 38
related commands, 72–73, 155
basename command
related commands, 69
summary of, 39
batch command
related commands, 57
summary of, 40
batching jobs, 40
bell parameter (ftp command), 82
Berkeley UNIX, 2, 3, 158
bibliography, 157–158
binary parameter (ftp command),
82
binary notations of access
permissions, 33–34, 49
block counts for files, 131
block-special files, 29
Bourne shell
about, 13–14
C shell and, 14–16
broadcasting messages, 151
BSD (Berkeley System Development)
evolution of, 2
features of, 3
online resources for, 158
buzz-builder shell script, 25–27
bye parameter (ftp command), 82
byte sequences of file system, 27–28

## C

-c parameter
for cc command, 45
for head command, 86
for pg command, 114

double greater-than symbol (>>),
        append indicator, 8, 44
du command
    related commands, 65
    summary of, 70–71

## E

-e parameter (pg command), 114
e parameter (ps command), 117
echo command
    related commands, 151, 155
    summary of, 72–73
egrep command
    related commands, 77, 85
    summary of, 74
e-mail, 96
    blocking messages, 99
    writing to all users, 151
ending processes, 89
ensuring uninterrupted commands,
        106
environment variables parameter
        (login command), 90
environment variables, 14
    mapping to station or PC, 75
    setting in C and Bourne shells,
        14–16
evolution of UNIX, 1–2
execute file access permissions,
        32–33
executing commands on remote
        systems, 146–147
export command, 75
expressions
    getting regular, 74, 77, 85

testing, 137–138
extracting columns from file, 61

## F

-f parameter
    for mv command, 102
    for pg command, 114
    for rm command, 121
    for rmdir command, 123
    for sort command, 126
-f string parameter (csplit
        command), 58
-f<list> parameter (cut command),
        61
-F field delimiter parameter (awk
        command), 37
\f parameter (echo command),
        72–73
f parameter (ps command), 117
false command
    related commands, 84, 140
    summary of, 76
fgrep command
    related commands, 74, 85
    summary of, 77
file1 parameter
    for cat command, 43
    for cmp command, 52
    for comm command, 53
    for cp command, 54
file1 parameter (diff command),
        66
file1 file2 parameter (join
        command), 88
file2 parameter

*(continued)*

# my2cents.idgbooks.com